THE VEGETABLE
GROWER'S HANDBOOK

THE VEGETABLE
GROWER'S HANDBOOK

Unearth your garden's full potential | HUW RICHARDS

CONTENTS

SEED STARTING AND TRANSPLANTING

HOW TO GROW CROPS

HERBS AND FLOWERS

COMMUNITY GARDENING

FOREWORD

Before writing this book, I thought long and hard about the direction I wanted to take. There is certainly an abundance of gardening books full of step-by-step instructions on how to grow different crops. However, information on the best ways to optimize the productivity of a vegetable garden isn't so easy to find. Therefore, my core purpose is to teach you the necessary skills, thought-processes, and strategies to get the most from your space.

You'll learn techniques for maintaining soil health, sowing seeds for maximum success, as well as which edible pollinator-friendly plants to grow, where to place your compost bins, and when to consider self-sufficiency. For each technique I'll explain not just how but why it works so you can make your own adjustments. Experience has shown me there is room for adaptation in almost every aspect of gardening so consider this book as a guide, not a rulebook. Having broken many "rules" in the garden and discovered it is more productive as a result, I feel passionately that every gardener should be free to develop their own growing style.

Creating the vegetable garden of your dreams is a constant process of adjustment and both you and the garden will evolve and grow together. You'll learn not only how to grow fantastic food but also how you can develop as a gardener by asking the right questions, learning the most effective skills, and always being open to experiment.

Whether you're just starting to grow your own food or a seasoned gardener looking for more, the aim of this book is to unearth and harness your garden's full potential.

SET YOUR
GARDEN GOALS

Find your motivation and follow the principles of organic gardening

ON A MISSION

KNOWING WHY YOU GARDEN

This book is about improving productivity and efficiency, and to get there we need to start by asking a very basic question: why do you garden? Knowing your "why" is essential for a gardening journey that will motivate and excite you.

FEELING A SENSE OF PRIDE EVERY TIME YOU READ OUT YOUR MISSION STATEMENT IS THE SIGN OF A GREAT ONE.

When there is too much to do in the garden, it's very easy to get derailed and lose sight of why you wanted to garden in the first place. I had a tough time a couple of years ago with so much going on that I almost forgot why I'd even started my growing journey and why I love gardening. Then one day, while taking a break, I realized that to reignite my passion I needed to create something that would focus my energy, keep me on track, and help me to achieve my gardening objectives. I felt it was time to create a personal gardening mission statement.

WHAT IS A MISSION STATEMENT?

A tool that is mostly associated with the business world, a mission statement is a summary of an organization's goals and values. To give you a better idea of what these entail, here are the mission statements of some well-known global brands:

- **Google** "To organize the world's information and make it universally accessible and useful."
- **Tesla** "To accelerate the world's transition to sustainable energy."
- **LinkedIn** "To connect the world's professionals to make them more productive and successful."

KEY ELEMENTS

I don't see why you can't create and apply a mission statement to any aspect of life. Put simply, it encapsulates your "purpose". When trying to come up with your own statement, it's a good idea to keep it to

one sentence and make it short and snappy. I think it should start with the word "to" because that immediately suggests something to work towards. Next comes your choice of verb because a mission statement is action-oriented and a meaningful verb helps you to visualize your goal. To give you an example, I'd like to share my current gardening mission statement:

"To escape from a busy world and relish every harvest."

My verb "escape" is simple to visualize and very personal to me. A couple of years ago, I rarely had time to switch off so this year I wanted gardening to be my escape – an opportunity to slow down and concentrate on being "present" in the garden. I added the second part "and relish every harvest" to remind myself to take the time to appreciate and celebrate every small success. Having a connecting phrase in your mission statement allows you to add another aspect that either backs up your verb or introduces an additional objective, like Google's aim to make information "universally accessible and useful". I can almost taste the phrase "and relish every harvest" every time I recall my statement!

CREATE YOUR STATEMENT

Trying to summarize your own gardening goals and values in a single sentence might sound challenging, but why not make a start? Set aside 30 minutes or so, sit down with a pen and paper, and think about your own gardening mission statement. Use the examples on the previous page for guidance and remember to keep it short, snappy, and forward-looking.

Begin by thinking of a verb that "speaks to you" and then see where this takes you. There is no right or wrong when it comes to a mission statement as long as it captures your passion and values. You also need to make the mission statement as personal to your situation as possible to really own it.

If you have a hard time finishing your mission statement in one session, sleep on it, and revisit it the following day. For me, that almost always does the trick! It's also a good idea to try out a few different versions until you find the one that resonates with you the most. Once you've decided on your bespoke mission statement, write it out big and bold and put it in a prominent place where you'll see it every day, such as on the bathroom mirror or above the potting bench.

THE AUTUMN REVIEW

Your mission statement shouldn't be set in stone for the foreseeable future and I recommend that you review it every autumn. Your experience over the previous growing season may mean making adjustments or even deciding on a new statement for the following year. An autumn review gives you plenty of time to plan next year in alignment with any new aspirations, so you are always reminded of why gardening and growing food is your passion. Adapting my mission statement every year to reflect what excites and motivates me the most is key to keeping me on track.

Before you make a big decision about your garden, think about it in the context of your mission statement. Does the decision make sense in the light of your situation and will it help you stay true to your goals and values? More often than not, the answer is "yes", but taking time to ensure you always keep your objectives in mind will prevent you from going too far off track. This book aims to help you garden smarter, and although creating a productive garden doesn't happen overnight, the simple steps I recommend will bring noticeable and lasting changes.

THE BOOK'S MISSION

When I set out to write *The Vegetable Grower's Handbook*, I knew from experience that a mission statement would define the book's ambition and help to focus my writing. I'd like to share it with you:

"To inspire you, the reader, to garden more efficiently and develop your own growing style so you can realize your goals."

Once you learn how best to spend the time available to you in the garden, you'll be better equipped to focus on creating a truly productive space and grow whatever inspires your passion. The methods I outline in this book have brought me abundant harvests and I hope they do the same for you.

Start each gardening session with a clear mind and if you stay true to your objectives you'll finish it with a real sense of satisfaction.

Even though your garden is a productive space, it's also a place where you can relax, leave the busy world behind, and take pleasure in what all your hard work has made possible.

PERMACULTURE

SUSTAINABLE GROWING

A system that takes its inspiration from the natural world, permaculture is the core influence on how I grow food. It's all about working in harmony with nature, rather than pushing against it.

WHAT IS PERMACULTURE?

A combination of two words, permanent and agriculture, permaculture is the brainchild of Australians Bill Mollison and David Holmgren who were looking for positive solutions to environmental destruction. They created a design system for growing food in abundance that was not only sustainable but would also regenerate the landscape by encouraging diversity, stability, and resilience. Its principles work on the micro and macro scale, and you can apply them to any garden or growing area.

To me, the reason why permaculture makes sense is that you're observing systems that work well in nature and then applying their principles on a practical level. For example, there is no waste in nature; every single thing has a purpose and a use. When you compost so-called "waste materials" from the garden and return them to the soil, that's permaculture in action.

Following permaculture principles, such as staying in tune with the local climate and making garden waste into compost, helps all my plants to flourish.

ETHICS AND PRINCIPLES

I like to think of permaculture's ethics and principles as "thought tools" that help unearth potential in any vegetable garden.

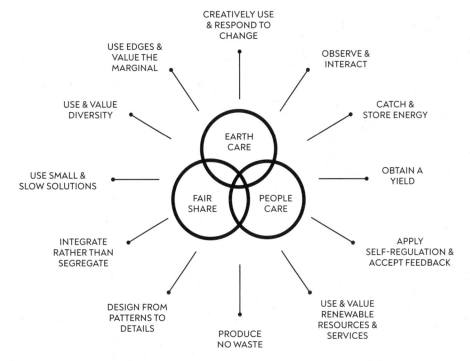

PERMACULTURE IS A VERY FLEXIBLE SYSTEM AND ANYONE CAN USE IT, WHATEVER THE SIZE AND SITUATION OF THEIR GARDEN, TO MAKE A POSITIVE DIFFERENCE.

A diagrammatic illustration of permaculture values with the three key ethics at the centre, surrounded by the 12 design principles.

THE THREE ETHICS
Permaculture has three key ethics at its core:
- **Earth care** (care for the soil and the planet)
- **People care** (care for ourselves and our community)
- **Fair share** (sharing space with nature alongside sharing surplus, ideas, and skills)

These guiding ethics are designed to ensure that how we grow food has the most positive impact possible. I like to turn them into the questions below and regularly check that I'm adhering to all three.
- Am I taking action to care for the planet?
- Am I taking action to care for myself, my family, friends, and community?
- Am I sharing not only garden gluts, but also skills and ideas with others?

THE 12 PRINCIPLES
From the three ethics, the 12 principles follow. To help you understand these I've provided practical examples of how I've responded to them in a question and answer format.

Creatively use and respond to change
What changes have you experienced, and how can you make the most of them?
Owing to recent summer droughts, I invested in second-hand IBC tanks. These store 6,000 litres (1,320 gallons) of emergency water, so I am well prepared for future drought.

Observe and interact

How or why did that happen, and what next?
Voles damaged my direct-sown swedes, but a crop started in modules fared much better. Could this be my go-to method for swedes?

Catch and store energy

What resources can you collect and store as a gardener that will be available when needed?
I put as much organic matter in my compost bin as possible. Once decomposed, this can be applied to my garden when needed.

Obtain a yield

How can you get a harvest, or improve the yield from a specific area?
Under the espalier fruit trees, there was unused space in a prime south-facing position so I lined some tyres and grew a crop of oca in them to maximize harvests.

Apply self-regulation and accept feedback

When is it time to go back to the drawing board? How can I source constructive criticism to find a solution or improvement?
Whenever I've tried and failed to deal with a new problem, I make online contact with gardeners in a similar climate to ask for advice. After mulling this over, I'm often able to come up with a solution.

Use and value renewable resources and services

What local resources can you use to lower costs and help grow healthier crops?
Woodchip can be used in compost, to mulch beds, or as a path surface. In many areas, tree surgeons will drop off piles for free.

Produce no waste

How do I make sure that I am making the most of every single harvest?
If I have excess tomatoes, I turn them into a sauce that can be frozen to enjoy a taste of summer in the depths of winter.

You can see permaculture principles in action in my garden from the diversity of plants grown to the crops around the edges and up vertical structures.

Design from patterns to details

What opportunities and drawbacks does my local climate provide?
In Wales, the abundant rainfall is ideal for brassicas and leafy greens. To avoid soil saturation and grow the broadest range of crops, I've created raised beds.

Integrate rather than segregate

How can I bring individual elements together to enjoy multiple benefits?
I grow different plants together whenever possible. When kale is underplanted with coriander and parsley, the partial shade stops the herbs running to seed too quickly, extending the harvesting period.

Use small and slow solutions

What are the small improvements I can make today, that will lead to significant returns?
The simplest task can result in noticeable changes. After sowing a tray of calendula in spring, I'll enjoy orange blooms all summer.

Use and value diversity

How can I ensure that I not only have a diverse range of plants, but also support nature's diversity?
I don't try to eradicate weeds and always let patches of nettles thrive. They are not only edible, but also the food source for many beneficial insects, such as butterfly caterpillars.

Use edges and value the marginal

How can I make the most of boundaries, pathways, and vertical structures?
Once I'd attached trellis to the perimeter fence, it became an effective and attractive wind barrier and opened up the possibility of tree crops, shade, and wildlife habitat.

Permaculture's core philosophy of working with nature means encouraging biodiversity, growing what suits your climate, and keeping the soil healthy. The 12 principles serve as tools to help you make the right decisions for you, your garden, and nature. In this book, you'll find many examples of the principles in action and I hope you will appreciate how useful they are in making your space more rewarding, sustainable and productive.

TIP

PERMACULTURE IS NOT A RULEBOOK. INSTEAD, CONSIDER IT A TOOL THAT HELPS YOU FOCUS ON CREATING POSITIVE CHANGE AND LONG-TERM STRATEGIES THAT BRING MULTIPLE BENEFITS BOTH TO YOU AND TO YOUR GARDEN.

THE NECESSITY OF DIVERSITY

INSPIRED BY NATURE

Growing a variety of plants is the key to a more productive, resilient, and sustainable vegetable plot. Discover how to increase the diversity of your garden and enjoy abundant, healthy crops.

TIP

COUNT HOW MANY PLANT SPECIES YOU CAN FIND IN A HEDGEROW OR WILDFLOWER MEADOW.

I always garden with nature in mind and one of the permaculture principles most deeply embedded in my approach to growing food is using and valuing diversity. Natural, unmanaged habitats feature a broad range of plant (and animal) species and this variation promotes healthy growth and development.

WHAT IS DIVERSITY?

Applying the principle of diversity to our gardens means growing a variety of food crops and other plants together. By doing this, we are creating a polyculture (see p154), as opposed to a monoculture (where one or very few species of plants are grown over a large area). In monocultures, once a problem has taken hold, an entire crop can be wiped out. Diversity in the planting of your plot, however, makes it more difficult for a pest or disease to target or spread to a particular crop.

THE BENEFITS OF DIVERSITY

A variety of plant species not only offer more protection against pests and diseases, they also make the garden more attractive to beneficial insects that will pollinate your crops and help to keep down pest numbers. The presence of a small number of pests, however, is not always a bad thing – and no garden can be entirely pest- or disease-free. To maintain a healthy population of beneficial insects, you need some pests around to provide a decent food source.

A garden that is planted with a range of different species has the potential to be rich in wildlife and abundant with healthy produce.

HOW TO ACHIEVE DIVERSITY

Below I outline various gardening techniques that will help you to cultivate diversity in all its forms. I like to apply all methods to create what I call "intensive diversity".

- Polyculture (p154)
- Intercropping (p156)
- Succession planting (p152)
- Growing ornamentals with edibles (pp186–197)
- Building healthy soil (pp44–71)
- Small-space mindset (pp170–173)
- Growing annuals with perennials (pp186–199)

You will find more detailed information related to specific pests and diseases on pages 134–141. However, I felt it was important to mention that many of the techniques you willl learn will, in themselves, help to prevent pest and disease issues while also making your garden more productive. Remember, in nature (and in some cases your garden), small numbers of pests and disease-causing organisms play a vital role in maintaining the populations of other crucial species that also fend them off. Nature always performs a fine balancing act.

Growing ornamentals in and around your plot is a great way to entice a vast array of beneficial insects for pest control and pollination.

The diversity of plants growing in this section of my vegetable garden:

A Blueberries
B Borage
C Cornflowers
D Cosmos
E Mint
F Lettuce
G Globe artichoke
H Oca
I French climbing beans
J Runner beans
K Nasturtiums
L Asparagus
M Sweet peas
N Peas
O Plums
P Potatoes

SKILLS
FOR EFFICIENCY

Techniques to keep you organized and realize your garden's potential

ORGANIZE AND PRIORITIZE

HOW TO KEEP THINGS RUNNING SMOOTHLY

Discover how to use checklists and to-do lists to stay on top of garden tasks and make the best use of your time. I'm also sharing the organization and prioritization strategies that help me manage busy periods in the garden.

Although your first instinct might be to just get outside and see what needs to be done, spending a few minutes focusing your energy will result in a more efficient and productive plot. If you want anything to run smoothly, good preparation and organization are key. Checklists and to-do lists show at a glance what needs to be done, as well as what advance prep might be necessary.

CREATE A ROUTINE CHECKLIST

Listing essential gardening tasks that you need to do on a regular basis helps you get into the flow of a routine. You will be referring to this list throughout the growing season and it's the best way of keeping on top of things – soon you will find yourself completing all tasks without any prompts as you become familiar with the checklist. Here is an example of a routine checklist I carry whenever I head to the garden during the growing season:

- Top up the water tanks
- Do a quick spot-check for any plant issues
- Check if seedlings need a water
- Spend 5 minutes doing a general weed
- Make sure all taps are off when I leave

Using and referring to this checklist lessens the likelihood of disasters, such as leaving the hose on and wasting vast amounts of water – a real disaster if, like me, you have no mains water supply! Start by sitting down with a pen and paper and listing six routine tasks. I recommend heading to your growing area so you can assess them in situ and add any tasks you may have missed. You'll be using

your checklist regularly, so make sure you note it down on something permanent so you can mentally "tick-off" tasks – I laminate mine! Alternatively, download a checklist app onto your phone and use that as reference.

TO-DO LISTS

My brain can often be a little chaotic, therefore having a simple tool in the form of a to-do list to capture all the tasks in one place helps keep me on track with the growing season. Every time I head to the garden I take a notepad with me and will spend a few minutes creating or updating my to-do list before I start a gardening session. You might want to draw up a list on a weekly basis, then either roll over any tasks still to be completed to the following week or start a fresh list. Whatever you decide, there is no right or wrong when it comes to creating a to-do list, as long as it's simple and you refer to it on a regular basis. My advice is to find a style that suits you best.

TIP

MAKE A SEPARATE WINTER CHECKLIST FOR MAINTENANCE JOBS, SUCH AS SHARPENING TOOLS.

Pausing for a few minutes on a busy July day to check progress on my to-do list.

WAYS OF PRIORITIZING

I rely on two strategies to help prioritize my to-do lists –
saving the best for last and batching.

SAVE THE BEST FOR LAST

Not knowing how to prioritize tasks and manage my time is something I have struggled with my whole life, often focusing on the wrong jobs and then running out of time to do the most crucial ones. As I was self-employed and juggling so many different projects, I knew I had to address the problem and manage my time much better. My own eureka moment came when I discovered a fascinating yet simple concept: start your day by doing the least enjoyable tasks first.

Why should the least enjoyable tasks be done first? Well, it all comes down to mindset. Jobs that you least want to do tend to loom large and bring up feelings of dread so we put them off. Unfortunately, they don't just go away. By just getting on with it and doing the least enjoyable tasks first, you can rid yourself of those looming negative feelings. For me, this means I often feel lighter, clearer-headed, and more confident in my decisions for the remainder of the day. To give you an example, I start with those annoying gardening tasks, such as weeding the perennial pots and then get on with the jobs I enjoy, such as transplanting seedlings.

Before your next visit to the garden, get out your to-do list, read through all the tasks and highlight any that you aren't keen on doing. Reorder these tasks with the least enjoyable first and the most enjoyable last.

TIP

COMPLETING THOSE MUNDANE JOBS ALLOWS YOU TO CLEAR YOUR MIND AND FOCUS MORE TIME AND ENERGY ON THE THINGS YOU LOVE DOING.

One of my least favourite garden jobs is spring cleaning the polytunnel, so I tackle that first.

BATCHING

Grouping similar tasks together and then focusing on completing one set at a time is what batching is all about. Although doing the least-enjoyable task first is an excellent strategy, sorting your tasks into groups according to location or function will also save you a lot of time and energy. When creating a list, such as the weekly to-do list (see p26), group the tasks into the most appropriate filter:

- **Filter 1** Location-based task (for example shed or polytunnel)
- **Filter 2** Function-based task (such as sowing)

After you've used the filters, you will suddenly see a chaotic to-do list become clearer and much more manageable.

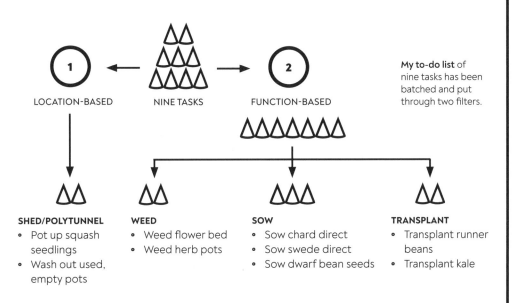

My to-do list of nine tasks has been batched and put through two filters.

LOCATION-BASED   **NINE TASKS**   **FUNCTION-BASED**

SHED/POLYTUNNEL
- Pot up squash seedlings
- Wash out used, empty pots

WEED
- Weed flower bed
- Weed herb pots

SOW
- Sow chard direct
- Sow swede direct
- Sow dwarf bean seeds

TRANSPLANT
- Transplant runner beans
- Transplant kale

TWO STRATEGIES AT ONCE

Now it's time to put into practice what you learned about prioritizing. Pick the batch that contains the task you dread the most, such as weeding the flower bed, and focus on completing this job before you move on to the remainder of the batch. Then continue to work through your batches in order of least-enjoyable task first. This way you'll be left with the most enjoyable batch last. It's always good to finish on a high!

Start any day in the garden watering seeds or seedlings – this always takes priority.

TWO 5-MINUTE FIXES

STRATEGIES FOR DEALING WITH OVERLOAD

Making checklists, prioritizing, and batching tasks are all great ways to stay in control but if you start to feel overwhelmed, a little extra help is needed. Make use of these excellent techniques to get yourself back on track.

TIP

COMPLETING A BUNCH OF FIVE-MINUTE JOBS IS A GREAT WAY TO HIT THE GROUND RUNNING BEFORE A NEW MONTH BEGINS.

1. THE FIVE-MINUTE JOB LIST

Towards the end of the month, I like to go into the garden and complete every single job I can think of that takes less than five minutes to complete. Having a big pile of "bitty" jobs can so easily trigger feelings of stress but making a set time every month to tick off a few of these small tasks can achieve big results. Take the weight off your shoulders by writing down a short list of five-minute jobs then head out and complete them.

Doing small jobs first will not only make you feel more productive but also put you in the right frame of mind to attempt the bigger tasks on your list. Remember, too, that, these tasks can be shorter than five minutes, but never longer! Often, before I tackle my main to-do list, I like to start a gardening session by getting a few five-minute jobs under my belt. To give you an example, these might include the following:

A. Weed around the brassica seedlings
B. Cut the growing tips off the runner beans
C. Transplant the radish seedlings
D. Water the under cover seedlings
E. Pinch out the tomato sideshoots
F. Tie up the sweet peas

2. THE FIVE-MINUTE CHALLENGE

We all feel resistance when approaching tricky tasks, but rather than put them to one side, why not take up the five-minute challenge? Start the job but tell yourself that if you're still not feeling motivated after five minutes then it's okay to stop and come back to it another time. The only downside to this approach is that you might lose five minutes of your time, which isn't much. Plus, you've already made a small start.

On the upside, there's a very good chance you'll carry on past the five-minute mark and complete the task – by far the hardest part is persuading yourself to take that first step. Once you push through this initial barrier, you regain focus and the procrastination issue is solved in just a few minutes.

STRESS-BUSTING STRATEGIES

If you feel close to overload, take a moment to explore why you feel this way and try your best to dig down to find the root cause. Remind yourself of your mission statement (see p12) and ask yourself if it's the right one for you and your garden or whether it might need adapting.

If you are feeling stressed most of the time, then you have probably taken on too much – a feeling I know well. Fortunately, there is a simple fix. All you need to do is put some areas of the garden to sleep by covering a raised bed with landscape fabric or cardboard and leaving it alone for the rest of the season. Once you feel you are back in control with time to spare, simply reawaken the sections of the garden you put to sleep and start growing in them again. The covering will ensure there won't be any weeds to remove and the bed will be ready for action, just as soon as you are.

HOW TO APPROACH BIG TASKS

BREAK IT DOWN AND SIMPLIFY

Large projects can spring up from time to time when growing your own food – here's how I approach them in order to overcome that daunting feeling and get the job done.

TIP

ANY COMPLEX PROJECT CAN BE REVERSE ENGINEERED INTO SIMPLE AND ACHIEVABLE STEPS.

How do you climb a mountain? The straightforward answer is "one step at a time", and this is exactly how a large task should be approached. The idea is to simply split something large into smaller bitesize chunks that are more manageable. Doing this tricks our brains into thinking the job is easier because there are lots of smaller tasks to complete, rather than one looming project.

REVERSE ENGINEERING

This principle of splitting up a large task can be applied to anything in life; in fact, my main breakthrough happened when I was writing *Veg in One Bed* and discovered a process called reverse engineering.

Working backwards from the end result, reverse engineering is taking something apart and analysing its components in detail to understand how it all comes together. You can apply this idea to cooking: for example, to get a cake, you need a recipe to follow from beginning to end to achieve the desired result. Think of garden projects as needing simplified recipes too. Methodically break a job down into easy steps until you have completed the whole task.

WHY USE THIS METHOD?

Often in gardening, the most straightforward approach is the best approach, and simplification makes anything easier to achieve. I find that the greatest benefit of using this method – splitting up a task into many micro-tasks – is that you get to enjoy plenty of quick wins as you progress. By creating a to-do list specifically for one big

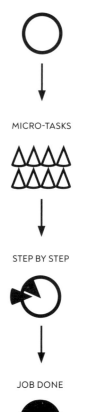

PROJECT

MICRO-TASKS

STEP BY STEP

JOB DONE

Break down your project into smaller tasks then tackle each, one step at a time.

task, you will have a lot of boxes to tick during the project, which provides a sense of achievement – often that is the only motivation you need to keep going! If you just had the entire project as one task on a to-do list, then it's hard to track progress, and the only real satisfaction you can enjoy is when the project is completed, which can feel a long way off at the beginning.

Another benefit of this approach is that to create a to-do list you need to carefully run through the process from start to finish in your head. In doing so, you can decide the most efficient way to order the smaller jobs, in terms of location, equipment, or technique. The other huge plus of running through the list of tasks in your head is that it provides the opportunity to identify possible pitfalls or issues you may come across when you're actually doing the job. You may discover that you have fewer screws than needed, or that you need to double-check the height of the fence posts required. Exploring and fixing potential issues before you have even started always makes for a smoother project and will result in as few hiccups as possible.

PUTTING IT INTO PRACTICE

Here are two example to-do lists showing how I have split one task into numerous quick wins.

TASK: CLEAR THE POLYTUNNEL FOR WINTER

- Pull out the old plants in the bed and place in a wheelbarrow
- Empty all the old pots and trays that still contain compost into the wheelbarrow
- Empty the contents of the wheelbarrow into a compost bin
- Fill the wheelbarrow with compost and lightly mulch both polytunnel beds
- Apply a wheelbarrow load of woodchip to the path
- Wipe down the inside of the polytunnel
- Wipe down the outside of the polytunnel
- Clear and wipe down the potting table
- Stack away all the pots under the bench

Note – I batched (see p29) the wheelbarrow jobs together and considered the location of the compost bin within the garden to save time and avoid multiple trips. If I am emptying a wheelbarrow of compost materials in the compost area, I may as well fill the wheelbarrow with fresh compost then and there to take back to the polytunnel.

TASK: PRUNE THE SOFT FRUIT

- Sterilize pruning tools
- Prune the blackcurrants
- Prune the row of redcurrants about the polytunnel
- Prune redcurrants under trees
- Prune the gooseberries
- Prune the trailing berries
- Clean and dry pruning tools
- Collect prunings for woody compost or bonfire

Note – Here, I am making sure I focus on one style of pruning at a time because different soft fruit crops require different pruning methods. I also choose to start with blackcurrants as they are the easiest to prune, which means I can get a quick-win under my belt. It's a good idea to gradually ease yourself in and have a real sense of progress as soon as possible (see p30). I finish by collecting prunings as it's satisfying to tidy up and I can also enjoy a bonfire with family and friends.

OBSERVE AND INTERACT

UNLOCK YOUR GARDEN'S POTENTIAL

Set aside time to look closely at your growing space and take in every detail. It's the best way to appreciate all its advantages as well as explore creative solutions to existing challenges.

This is my favourite of the 12 core principles of permaculture, a design system of growing food sustainably that uses nature as its inspiration. Through close observation we gain a better, more in-depth understanding of our gardens, which enables us to follow through with adjustments and improvements.

Many gardens have a fantastic amount of hidden potential, and observation and interaction is a great tool for unlocking it. Bill Mollison, the "father" of permaculture, developed a philosophy of working with nature not against it and as gardeners, we can get so much more from our space if we play to its inherent strengths. But it takes time to appreciate fully what these strengths are and discover ways of using them to our advantage.

WHEN IT COMES TO GARDENING, I'M ALWAYS LOOKING TO LEARN, NOT JUST FROM FAILURES BUT ALSO FROM SURPRISES.

EXPERIMENTS AND PROBLEM SOLVING

I apply the observe and interact principle in two instances: to test out new ideas or techniques and tackle garden challenges.

When experimenting with new materials or growing techniques, I observe how well they work and then come up with any necessary adjustments. I also apply the principle to existing challenges, such as an overexposed site or my disappointing carrot crops. Once I notice something that's not quite working, I consider what factors are at play and think about how the issue might be solved. Below, I've set out the formulas I use in both instances and these are followed by two examples: the first is an experiment and the second a longstanding issue which I needed to address.

EXPERIMENTAL
- Come up with idea
- Test the idea
- Observe what happens
- Tweak if necessary

CHALLENGE BASED
- Recognize challenge
- Understand why it exists
- Create a solution
- Observe results if it wasn't successful

Tweak or alter the solution (if close to overcoming the challenge)

Abandon and try a different solution (if it makes no difference)

After the success of trialling growing runner beans up one IBC tank, I have decided to grow them up all six tanks around the garden.

EXPERIMENT WITH RUNNER BEANS

After planting out the young runner beans, I was left with spare seedlings and decided to grow them up the big IBC tank (bulk liquid tank from agricultural suppliers) that we use to store water at the top of the garden. The seedlings were planted in a container at the base of the tank two weeks later than the main crop and were all rootbound. As both sets of runner beans grew, I observed progress in both locations and compared their performance. To my surprise, the runner beans on the tank were ready to harvest two weeks before the main crop even though they were planted out later. After thinking this through, I realised that the white colour of the tank reflected light onto the plants, while the thermal mass of the water inside retained heat overnight. It was the combination of increased light and warmth that helped the plants develop and fruit sooner. Having made this discovery, I will now always grow runner beans and other climbers up IBC tanks for years to come.

EXPOSED-SITE CHALLENGE

Sticking with the subject of runner beans, I had a dilemma when it came to which vertical structure was best for dealing with wind. Through past experience, we know that one section of the vegetable garden is exposed to gusts from the adjoining field so I decided to construct an A-frame for the beans to act as a wind barrier. I was curious to see how the bean structure would perform, having assumed that tying it to the raised bed at both ends would provide strength. In fact, everything was working exceptionally well until we had an August storm and the wooden structure collapsed completely! I observed that the A-frame structure was easily blown over because it acted like a sail. So, it was back to the drawing board. Instead, I opted to grow runner beans on a wigwam as the wind is able to pass through these more easily. So far, these structures are holding firm and I am thrilled that I am now able to grow tall crops in this exposed part of the garden.

5-MINUTE OBSERVATION EXERCISE

Take a break with a pen and notepad, and jot down ideas as you look around different places in your garden.

QUESTION AND VISUALIZE

I love to have a really good look around when stopping for a 5-minute tea break in the garden. As you observe the area in front of you, start asking yourself "What if?" and let your imagination run free. What if the raised-bed paths were narrower? What if I set up a water butt to collect the rainwater from the woodshed? What if I could create a chicken compost area on the other side of this fence? What if I planted parsley in-between the runner bean seedlings? Visualization is a powerful tool because it helps us to think creatively and embrace possibilities. When ideas or images come up that excite you, and you think might work, write them down on a notepad, along with the emotion they inspire. You'll soon feel motivated to try something new or put in the hard work to make some improvements.

PLAN AHEAD

After doing this observation exercise a few times a week, you'll have a growing list of ideas for making the most of your space, as well as for planting possibilities. When to interact and put your ideas into practice is, of course, down to you and how much time you have available. The formulas on the previous two pages will help you think through any changes you'd like to make and also to assess the results when you put them into practice. If you're contemplating DIY-based projects or making long-term changes, winter is the perfect time to revisit your list, and always remember to break down big tasks into simple steps.

REPURPOSING UNUSED SPACES

Many of us have a challenging spot that, with a little imagination, could be put to much better use. I've often taken 5 minutes to focus on areas of my garden that had the potential to be more productive, especially those out-of-the-way corners.

Here are some suggestions for increasing the productivity of those unused or overlooked spaces in the garden:

• Position a water butt or large container to collect and store water. Dunk a watering can in it for irrigation; it's more efficient than filling the can from a tap.

• Grow edible climbers in large containers up the sides of fences, posts, sheds, walls, or water storage tanks.

• Make space for two or three compost bins – corners that don't get much sun or the shady side of a polytunnel are ideal spots.

• Grow small fruit trees along your boundary or fix trellis along a fence for training vertical perennial crops.

• Construct a simple wire cage to collect and store fallen leaves to make leaf mould.

Recently, I transformed a corner of my plot by installing an IBC tank next to the polytunnel. This made watering the crops inside much easier. Realizing I could take this further, I propped up pallets along the sides of the tank, lining the gaps and filling them with compost. Planted with salad leaves and edible annuals, the pallets added vertical growing space as well as welcome colour.

TIP

IT'S VITAL TO ADAPT YOUR GARDEN OVER TIME. EVERYTHING CHANGES AND WE MUST WORK WITH OUR GARDEN EVERY STEP OF THE WAY.

Standing pallets up against the sunny side of my water tank and planting them with salad leaves and annual flowers looks attractive, as well as providing overnight warmth to aid growth.

TOWARDS MINIMALISM

THE DOWNSIDE OF HAVING MORE CHOICE

I watched a fascinating TED talk titled "The Paradox of Choice" by Barry Schwartz who outlined why too much choice can be problematic. It motivated me to limit my gardening choices and I'll explain why this has proved so beneficial.

PURPOSEFULLY GIVING MYSELF LESS CHOICE IN CERTAIN AREAS HAS MADE A HUGE, POSITIVE IMPACT ON MY GARDENING JOURNEY.

Having more choice is often considered a sign of greater freedom, but this can come at a cost. The first major downside is that too much choice can induce paralysis because we simply can't decide which is the best out of the many options presented to us. Yet if we overcome our paralysis and make a choice, we risk being disappointed because too many options tend to increase our expectations. Inevitably, whatever we choose tends to fall short and we ask ourselves whether we made the wrong decision. If you've ever been confronted by a large, complicated menu when eating out, you'll know exactly what I mean!

KEEPING IT SIMPLE

Rather than adopting a truly minimalist style of growing, I try to make things simpler and more streamlined. Below are areas where limiting choice will lead to greater efficiency.

Tools

Over the years I have accumulated a huge range of garden tools, most of which I rarely use and take up valuable space. Put any tools you use and can't do jobs effectivley without to one side. At the end of the season you'll be surprised by how few tools you use regularly. Swap, sell, or gift the others.

Pots

For propagation, I generally use just four types of module tray sourced from one supplier (see Resources, p216). The choice has been deliberately restricted to meet my needs yet make seed sowing very efficient. I always have spare single pots and a few cell trays on hand for flexibility.

Seeds

At the end of the growing season, I like to prioritize seeds closest to their sow-by date and swap any spares and excess packets. Given the vast choice, you can also simplify the process of sourcing next season's seeds by sticking with one or two recommended suppliers (see Resources, p216).

Compost

I'm a strong advocate of making your own compost (see pp52–65) as it puts brown and green waste to good use, replenishing the soil. But if you don't have the space or choose to buy it ready-made, I recommend trying out a few different brands of peat-free compost to find the one that suits you best, and then buy only that brand. You know you'll get consistently good quality compost and results. Also, consider buying bulk bags to reduce plastic and cost.

Gardening books

Most of us will admit to having too many gardening books! Why not sort through them every year and donate those you rarely look at to a local charity shop or growing project?

Plug plants

Rather than trying to start everything from seed, it is easier to purchase plug plants for crops you may not want so much of, such as chilli peppers.

TIP

CHOOSE ONE SEED
COMPANY FOR
YOUR STAPLES AND
ANOTHER FOR THE
MORE UNUSUAL
OR RARE CROPS
THEN YOU CAN
ENJOY THE BEST
OF BOTH WORLDS.

Sometimes it's easier to keep things simple and dedicate a whole bed to a single crop, such as potatoes (*above*). Spread cardboard over an unused bed until you're ready to plant (*right*).

MANAGING GROWING SPACE

Try these options when you don't know where to start or have taken on too much.

• **Option 1** Bulk plant a staple crop, such as onions or potatoes. These take up a lot of space, allowing you to focus your attention on a smaller area. Share any gluts with family, friends, and neighbours.

• **Option 2** Put some space to bed by mulching lightly with compost and covering it with weighed-down cardboard (see p68). When you feel ready to take on that growing space, it will be all set for planting. No matter if the growing season is in full swing, simply press pause after harvesting.

THE GARDENER'S NOTEBOOK

A MUST-HAVE FOR EVERY GROWER

Your notebook is not for jotting down to-do lists. It is a precious and very personal resource for recording ideas for your outdoor space, noting down discoveries, sketching out plans, and capturing dreams.

" "

A GARDEN NOTEBOOK HELPS CURATE YOUR DISCOVERIES AND KICK-START YOUR DREAMS.

When gardening I always carry one invaluable tool – my notebook. Of course, you could use your phone as a notebook, but for me putting pen to paper is a more meaningful, tactile process. And on a practical level, I find it much easier to flick through a notebook than scroll through various phone notes.

CREATIVE ASSISTANT

Use your notebook as a "brain dump" for writing down the various thoughts that arise naturally while you're gardening. Or think of it as a "creative assistant", an aid to exploring and refining your ideas so you unlock your space's potential and get the most enjoyment from your garden. The first thing to do is invest in a good-quality product that will last and that feels great in your hands. You'll value it more than a regular notepad and be motivated to use and look after it. I'm always excited by the prospect of filling my notebook because the information will be invaluable in helping me to improve my garden space.

GET INTO THE HABIT

Before I started using a notebook, a great idea would often pop into my head while gardening. I'd promise myself I would write it down later only to forget all about it! So, get into the habit of taking your notebook with you every time you go to the garden, and put pen to paper while the idea is still fresh in your mind. Personally, I put the date at the top right of each page so I can quickly flick through the months, but you might prefer to use numbers or some other system.

A notebook is also essential when visiting other gardens. Write down whatever inspires you and jot down any ideas that you might be able to adapt and tweak for your own garden. Also, why not take it to local or national horticultural shows where you might see an unusual variety of vegetables or fruit that you'd like to try?

PLANNING AND REFERENCE

In winter, when you've set aside time to create a planting plan for the following year, you'll find the gardener's notebook is the perfect reference tool for the job. Before making any plans, I recommend you read through the whole of your notebook (or notebooks if you write a lot) so you can pinpoint and focus on those key ideas and goals that will help shape the direction you take in the next growing season. And further down the line you will probably revisit previous notebooks from time to time, to refresh your memory and track the progress of your growing journey.

I often sketch in my notepad to help visualize my ideas and bring them to life.

ALWAYS KEEP YOUR
OLD NOTEBOOKS
SAFE SO YOU DON'T
LOSE VALUABLE
INFORMATION.

SOIL
AND COMPOST

Nurture the soil and reap the benefits with healthy and abundant crops

HEALTHY SOIL

RESPECT LIFE UNDERGROUND

As an organic gardener, soil health is my number one priority. Even growing vegetables comes second because the health of the soil has such a direct impact on the crops we grow. Get the soil right and you will enjoy better harvests.

TIP

INCREASE EARTHWORM POPULATIONS AND IMPROVE SOIL STRUCTURE BY MULCHING BEDS WITH COMPOST, LEAF MOULD, FINELY CHOPPED PLANT MATTER, OR GRASS CLIPPINGS.

WHAT IS HEALTHY SOIL?

In this chapter, I want to explore the key principles and techniques for creating and nurturing a healthier soil. But first, we need to take a closer look at the composition of soil and the amazingly diverse life within it that supports plant growth.

The structural foundation of soil is a mix of minerals (from broken-down rocks), organic matter, air, and water. That may sound straightforward, but soil is one of the most complex and diverse ecosystems known to science and teems with life on a microscopic scale. A single teaspoon of soil can contain up to one billion bacteria, of which there are many thousands of species, as well as several metres of mycorrhizal fungi threads called hyphae (microscopic fungi roots) that grow throughout the soil.

Organic material in the soil is a reservoir of water and nutrients made from live, dead, or decaying plant and animal matter that plants absorb with the help of bacteria, fungi, earthworms, and other organisms.

UNDERGROUND SUPPORT SYSTEMS

In a healthy soil, bacteria and fungi provide plants with nutrients and water in exchange for sugars and other organic substances that the plants release from their roots. This symbiotic relationship benefits all parties – plants, bacteria, and fungi – which work together in harmony. Earthworms also assist with the take-up of nutrients by creating tunnels that improve soil drainage and airflow – this benefits aerobic bacteria that need oxygen to survive.

Bacteria

Most bacteria in the soil are decomposers, which means they break down organic material (usually fresh plant matter) into nutrients. These are subsequently released into the soil once the bacteria die or are consumed by another soil organism, such as a nematode (a microscopic worm-like animal). Compared with the complex carbons found in old organic material, fresh plant matter tends to be rich in simple sugars, such as glucose, which bacteria find easy to digest so it is often their primary food source. Some of the glucose plants create from photosynthesis is transported down to the rhizosphere – the narrow zone where their roots meet the soil. At this level, bacteria (called rhizobacteria) are particularly abundant and they perform two core functions. Firstly, they break down organic compounds to make nutrients available for nearby roots to absorb. Secondly, they act as a natural defence system by forming a protective barrier around the roots that prevents diseases entering the plant.

Fungi

Bacteria are, however, unable to transport nutrients from elsewhere in the soil directly to a plant's roots and when a plant can't source nutrients, issues such as lower yields and reduced resistance to pests and diseases become apparent above ground. But this is where mycorrhizal fungi come in. They attach their microscopic hyphae to the plant's roots, effectively extending the plant's root system to allow the mining of necessary nutrients.

Mycorrhizal fungi found under a pallet plank that I used to help germinate my carrot seedlings. These fungi are a great indicator of healthy soil.

Although plants have fine roots for absorption – usually around 0.2mm thick – those of mycorrhizal hyphae have a diameter of just 2–20 micrometres (1,000 micrometres = 1 millimetre). While plant roots are able to access soil cavities called macropores, hyphae are small enough to enter tiny micropores, which is where the majority of nutrients and water are found. Fungi use enzymes to break down complex compounds in organic matter, digesting nutrients that are transported throughout the hyphae and often end up at the roots of plants. Here, they exchange substances such as phosphorus, water, and nitrogen for secretions from the plant roots in a process that benefits both fungi and plant. Fungi also help plants to source additional moisture from the soil, making the plants more resilient in periods of dry weather.

Earthworms

The humble earthworm, or "nature's plough", feeds on plant debris found on the surface of the soil and moves it below the surface, releasing nutrient-rich castings. Often these castings are left in worm tunnels, and these tunnels function as passageways for plant roots, hyphae, water, and air to travel through. These tunnels significantly improve soil structure so if high numbers of earthworms are active in your garden soil, your crops will certainly benefit.

DOS AND DON'TS

I have only just scratched the surface of the wonderful world of soil but I want to make it crystal clear that plants do not function independently. To thrive, they need to be part of an ecosystem that is rich in soil biology, including bacteria and mycorrhizal fungi. Applying synthetic fertilizers, spraying pesticides, double digging, and not protecting the soil, however, will all contribute to the destruction of this vital microbial life. Bacteria, fungi, and earthworms are our fellow gardeners; in this chapter, I'll show you no-dig and composting methods that support soil health and result in a more productive vegetable garden.

WHEN A TREE FORMS A SYMBIOTIC RELATIONSHIP WITH MYCORRHIZAL FUNGI, IT EFFECTIVELY EXTENDS THE SURFACE AREA OF ITS ROOTS BY A COLOSSAL 700 TO 1,000 TIMES!

NO-DIG GARDENING

MULCH YOUR WAY TO HEALTHY SOIL

Digging soil to grow food damages soil structure and impairs its ability to take up and retain moisture. Take digging out of the equation and soil health soon begins to improve, as thousands of gardeners and allotmenteers can testify.

NO-DIG IS THE SINGLE GREATEST GRASSROOTS GARDENING REVOLUTION OF RECENT TIMES.

WHAT IS NO-DIG?

Included under this broad term are gardening methods that improve soil health and structure by applying organic matter to the surface, rather than digging or forking it in. The organic materials used vary, but hay, leaves, woodchip, and compost are all popular. American organic gardener, Ruth Stout, swore by her "no-dig no-work" method of growing food. She used a permanent mulch of hay to suppress weeds and retain moisture while slowly adding organic matter to the soil as the mulch decomposed. Ruth encouraged people to put anything compostable straight onto the ground rather than let it break down first in a compost bin, and her methods attracted many followers – and a few sceptics.

In 2017 I trialled the "Stout" method and experienced mixed results. The potatoes did fantastically well, as did the kale, but the squash seedlings were hit hard by slugs. I planted out seven seedlings and thought they'd all been eaten until three came back with a vengeance and produced prolifically. I concluded that adding a permanent mulch is a viable method, but only if you garden in a drier climate where slugs are less of an issue, like Connecticut where Ruth Stout lived.

Another no-dig method, called "Back to Eden" gardening, was pioneered by American Paul Gautschi. He uses only composted wood chippings to mulch annual crops, while opting for fresher woodchip mulches for perennials. I've trialled this method with great results, while also using fresher woodchip as a mulch for annuals growing in raised beds with sides. To garden organically you need to source non-toxic woodchip and then let the pile break down for a year or two, which may be tricky if you have a small garden with no storage capacity. That said, I believe we as gardeners are yet to fully realize the potential woodchip has to offer.

BEST FOR MULCHING

The no-dig material of choice is compost without a doubt, especially in wetter climates such as the UK's because it is less attractive to slugs than materials such as hay, and so results in fewer crop disasters and better yields. Its one big advantage is that you can easily make your own for free or at very little cost from a wide variety of different materials (see pp52-55).

This whole book is based around the no-dig method of growing and compost is the primary material I use in the garden because it is so easy to work with. For the best outcome, a simple rule of thumb is to ensure you mulch the surface of your raised beds with at least 2–3cm (¾–1⅛in) of compost on an annual basis. You can do this at any time of year and in either full or empty beds.

Learn more about other materials suitable for mulching on page 142.

Mulching young kale plants with compost helps to retain moisture and adds all-important organic matter to the soil.

You can see just how **bountiful** and clean harvests are when crops are grown following no-dig principles. And not having to scrub off a hard crust of mud before I cook spuds is a blessing!

KEY BENEFITS OF NO-DIG

Using the no-dig method brings a multitude of benefits that gardeners can enjoy right away. The top five are listed below.

Less effort

No digging required! Instead of incorporating compost by digging or mixing it in, you simply spread it as a mulch over the surface of your growing area. Mulching is much quicker and less labour intensive than using a fork or spade.

Fewer weeds

Digging the soil disturbs its structure and brings weed seeds up to the surface where they germinate. No-dig effectively reduces their numbers and any weeds that do sprout are easily dealt with by hand-weeding or hoeing (see p132).

Cleaner harvests

Having used both traditional and no-dig methods to grow crops on heavy clay soil, I can testify that root vegetables come out of the ground cleaner when the soil has not been dug.

Drought resilience

By applying a surface mulch of compost you are effectively adding a protective layer to the soil beneath. The high percentage of organic matter in the compost helps to capture and retain moisture, which means you don't need to water your plants as often.

Flexibility

After applying the minimum 2–3cm (¾–1⅛in) layer of compost every year, you are good to go. The timing is entirely up to you but I like to apply mulch in late autumn or late winter, when there is less to do. Leave the mulch undisturbed and the ground will be ready for the new growing season.

TRANSITIONING TO NO-DIG GARDENING

If you're growing food in raised beds that you currently dig over or fork compost into, then autumn or winter is a good time to start the transition. Make sure the beds are well weeded and then apply a layer of at least 5cm (2in) of compost over the surface. When spring arrives, rake gently over the surface to create a tilth and then sow or transplant directly into it and grow on as usual (see pp86–89). After the first season you need to maintain no-dig beds by applying a 2–3cm (¾–1⅛in) layer of compost on a yearly basis. That is all it takes to transition – it couldn't be easier!

LONG-TERM STRATEGY

It's a misconception that no-dig requires more compost than traditional gardening. Yes, you will need a good amount in year one, but after that a 2–3cm (¾–1⅛in) layer of compost is all that is needed, and often this is the same or less than what is recommended to be forked or dug in. In addition, there are fantastic biological and mineral feeds you can make for little or no cost (see pp140–141 and pp178–181). Their short-term benefits will give a real boost to your plants so you enjoy abundant crops.

The single biggest asset to any garden is compost and in the following pages I explain how to make no-nonsense compost, create an efficient composting system, and discuss ways of sourcing extra material so you will be self-sufficient in nutrients and no longer need to buy compost, plant food, or fertilizer.

TIP

NO-DIG PRINCIPLES APPLY TO BOTH UNDER COVER AND OUTDOOR GROWING.

Following no-dig and returning organic matter to the soil gives me abundant, healthy growth and fantastic harvests.

NO-NONSENSE COMPOSTING

MINIMAL EFFORT REQUIRED

From hot composting to chickens, there are many ways to make compost.

Although it's important to find one that works for you, I'd like to share my go-to,

"lazy" system which has always given me consistently good results.

ESSENTIALS FOR LAZY COMPOST

There are just a few key requirements when making high-quality compost the easy way.

RIGHT BIN SIZE

The sides of the bin should be at least 1m (3ft) in length and height. This ensures the volume of material in the bin is sufficient for a core to form, which will generate and retain heat to speed up the composting process. Smaller bins don't allow enough heat to build up so they take an age to make compost. A bin that measures at least 1m x 1m (3 x 3ft) may seem large, especially if you have a small space, but you can always grow plants up the side and make a pallet lid so containers can sit on the top. A bin of that size will produce enough compost to mulch approximately four or five 1.2m x 3m (4ft x 10ft) raised beds. The bin should also have good airflow to avoid anaerobic decomposition, which slows down the process and can make the contents pretty smelly. A bin made from wooden slats or pallets is ideal.

RIGHT INGREDIENTS

When composting, there are two categories of ingredients – green and brown. Green materials are high in nitrogen and often in moisture content – properties which facilitate decomposition – while brown materials are high in carbon and have low moisture content. Striking the right balance of both types of material creates high-quality compost.

Green materials
- Used coffee grounds and plastic-free teabags
- Weeds without seedheads
- Fruit and vegetable scraps
- Lawn clippings
- Horse and cow manure
- Freshly-cut plant material
- Comfrey and nettles
- Seaweed
- Spent brewery grain (from a local brewery)
- Hair clippings (from barbers/hairdressers)
- Wool

Brown materials
- Dust from vacuuming
- Cardboard and newspaper
- Chippings and sawdust (from untreated wood)
- Autumn leaves
- Hay and straw
- Autumn and winter woody prunings
- Fallen pine needles
- Wood ash
- Tissues and paper towels
- Spent compost (from this-season's containers)

The greater the variety of green and brown materials, the more balanced your compost will be.

TIP

TO ACHIEVE GREAT COMPOST, YOU NEED THE RIGHT SIZE OF BIN AND A VARIETY OF APPROXIMATELY 50% GREEN MATERIAL AND 50% BROWN MATERIAL.

The vegetables and plant scraps (*above*) form a layer of green material that I usually cover with either cardboard (*bottom left)*, or autumn leaves (*bottom right)*. These browns balance out the nitrogen-rich greens.

TIP

SOME INGREDIENTS ARE BOTH GREEN AND BROWN, SUCH AS USED CHICKEN OR RABBIT BEDDING: THE MANURE IS THE GREEN ELEMENT AND THE BEDDING IS THE BROWN.

KEEP MATERIAL VARIED

The key to lazy composting is to add as many different ingredients (green and brown) as possible. Incorporating just a few materials means there is a risk the compost won't be balanced, both in terms of nutrients and pH (acidity or alkalinity). Aim to have a rough balance between green and brown material in terms of volume, and always include a good variety of both. For example, if you have a lot of green plant material to compost, keep the bin contents diverse by adding other green ingredients such as manure or coffee grounds plus a similar quantity of brown material at the same time.

FULL COMPOST BIN

Compost bins can be deceptive – they accommodate a much larger volume of material than you might think. Even when they look completely full, there is usually room to add more. Once the material has reached the top of the bin and is threatening to overflow, it's time to compress the contents so you can add more to the pile. One option is to place cardboard over the top of the compost, weight it with bricks or stones then wait a few days for the contents to settle. My preferred method is much easier – I simply walk over the top of the heap a few times to compact everything down. Ensuring your bin is filled to maximum capacity means you won't be left disappointed when the compost is ready and you find the pile has shrunk to a third of its original size!

Once the compost bin is completely full, I like to place a covering over the top. This not only helps shed excess rainwater but also reminds me not to add anything else to it.

WHEN IS COMPOST READY?

My lazy method will provide you with ready compost in around six months, depending on the season as well as the materials used. Some people like to turn the pile every couple of months and this can help the decomposition process, but it isn't really necessary and I tend to just leave the pile alone. Compost is ready when it has a lovely, fresh earthy smell – like a vibrant forest floor – and the texture is coarse but crumbly. Some twigs and leaves that have not fully broken down may still be visible but this doesn't affect the quality and is nothing to worry about.

Although this lazy compost still has a little way to go before it is fully decomposed, I will happily use it on my vegetable beds in autumn and winter.

ROUGHLY
CHOPPING UP
MATERIALS FOR
YOUR LAZY-METHOD
COMPOST BIN
WILL REDUCE
DECOMPOSITION
TIMES BY A MONTH
OR TWO.

WILDLIFE IN THE BIN

Rats

People are often discouraged from starting composting because they fear a bin might bring rats into the garden. Rats usually visit bins where cooked food, dairy and/or meat are present but these ingredients should not be composted and are not included in the list of green or brown materials (see p52). If there is nothing in there for a rat to eat, your compost bin is unlikely to become a rat magnet. Rats may well seek out a warm compost bin in a cold winter, but wouldn't you prefer to have one in your bin rather than it attempting to get into your house? Rats are going to be around whether you have a compost bin or not, but if you're still concerned then site your compost area at

Finished compost is crumbly, fresh-smelling and a pleasure to handle with just a few big pieces of material visible.

the far end of your garden, or consider investing in a rat-proof compost bin.

Beneficial wildlife

Not all creatures that you find in the compost bin are unwelcome in the garden. Slow worms and toads may also seek shelter in the warmth. If you come across one, move it carefully (especially during hibernation) to a safe space – it will return the favour by reducing numbers of troublesome garden pests, particularly slugs.

MULTI-BIN COMPOSTING

SYSTEMS TO IMPROVE EFFICIENCY

To my mind, a composting setup is essential for growing food and will ensure your soil and plants stay healthy. Space will dictate how many bins you can accommodate, but a three-bin system is productive enough for many gardens.

COMPOST IS AN ASSET THAT HOLDS VALUE. THINK OF MAKING COMPOST AS A NO-RISK INVESTMENT AND TRY TO GET INTO A POSITION WHERE YOU ALWAYS HAVE IT ON HAND.

For large growing areas, making enough compost for the whole garden will require a lot of effort. You might prefer to source bulk supplies of high-quality compost or at least supplement homemade compost with bought-in material. The principal benefit of homemade compost is that nutrients from plants that grew in your soil are returned directly to it, which creates a closed cycle. This builds up the health and resilience of both your soil and your plants.

EASY THREE-BIN SYSTEM

This method employs three bins of equal size, each containing material at a different stage in the composting process. The bins can be positioned next to each other or separated.

In a traditional three-bin system, material is moved from one bin to the next as it breaks down but here it stays put, although you can turn the contents. When one bin is full, simply close it off, leave for a few months to break down, and start filling the next bin.

Three stages

This system works on a rotation and your goal is to have a bin on the go for each stage:
- **Stage 1:** Bin (A) in process of being filled
- **Stage 2:** Closed bin (B) left to decompose
- **Stage 3:** Full bin (C) of compost that's ready to use.

It's a great routine to adopt, even if the timings won't always synchronize perfectly. For example, if your three bins are full, empty the one with compost at the most advanced stage of decomposition. Put the contents

into old compost bags and store them in a sheltered place. You now have an empty bin and can start the process again at Stage 1 by adding green and brown materials.

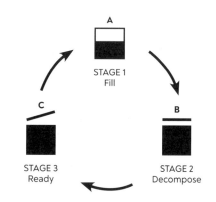

Bins A, B, and C are shown with compost at different points in the cycle. When compost is emptied out of Bin C at Stage 3, that bin reverts to Stage 1.

MORE SPACE, MORE BINS

For those with larger gardens and plenty of space, I'd suggest starting with at least four bins. You can then add more bins if the compost from four doesn't meet your annual requirements. I use a mix of homemade compost and bulk bought-in compost in my growing area. However, each year I'm actively increasing production of homemade compost to reduce my dependence on external sources.

I concentrate all my energy on filling one bin at a time using the no-nonsense method I described earlier (see pp52–55). My priority is to fill this as soon as possible because the sooner a bin is full, the sooner the contents break down into valuable compost. Later in this chapter I share my strategies for smarter sourcing of additional compostable materials so you always have enough to fill up your bins quickly (see p64).

My four-bin setup is situated between the house and garden. Each bin contains material at a different stage from half-filled to full and closed off.

TIP

MAKE THE MOST OF SPACE ABOVE AND AROUND COMPOST BINS BY GROWING CLIMBING PLANTS UP THE SIDES, PLANTING SQUASH IN FILLED BINS, OR CREATING A LID USING A PALLET THAT ALLOWS YOU TO PUT CONTAINERS ON TOP.

CHICKEN COMPOST

QUALITY MATERIAL FROM THE HEN COOP

Keep a few chickens in your garden and the coop can double up as an area for generating high volumes of compost, which is a fantastic use of space. Chickens also speed up composting by pecking at and mixing up garden waste.

TIP

SCATTERING CHICKEN FEED OVER THE COMPOSTING PILE WILL GIVE THE BIRDS AN EXTRA OPPORTUNITY TO SCRATCH AND MIX UP THE MATERIAL.

Chickens are expert composters: they peck, scratch, eat, and then digest waste green material. Combined with litter from the coop and other low-cost ingredients, their manure makes rich compost that you can use to grow fantastic crops. Chicken manure is high in nitrogen and phosphorous and also contains a respectable amount of potassium – all key elements for growing healthy vegetables. If you need a lot of compost, it's worth finding a regular source of ingredients to add to the pile. Establishing when supplies can be picked up or delivered will help with advance planning so you don't run short.

As I've already explained, good-quality compost is a mix of green and brown materials and the high nitrogen (green) content of chicken manure must be balanced by adding brown (carbon-rich) materials. I recommend you establish a good source of woodchip, spent hay or straw, and dried leaves so you can add these at the same time as other green material, such as grass clippings. Aim for around 50/50 green and brown material, but don't worry if you have a bit more of either.

DEEP MULCH COMPOSTING METHOD

Set up an area in the chicken run and adapt the guidelines below to find a system that suits you and your hens.

Materials and tools
- Three 60cm x 1.5m (2ft x 5ft) lengths of scrap wood, such as old boards
- Two 60cm (2ft) corner posts
- Hammer
- Nails
- Three 1.5m x 1.5m (5ft x 5ft) pieces of cardboard
- Bucket (suggested size: 14-litre/3 gallons)
- Pitchfork
- Spade
- 2 large stones

Chicken compost ingredients
- Weeds
- Shredded brown leaves
- Grass clippings (be conservative with quantities)
- Deciduous woodchip (avoid toxic species such as black walnut)
- Shredded prunings
- Used bedding from the chicken coop
- Spent hay or straw
- Plant material from the garden

1. Set aside a square or rectangle of ground within your chicken run. If you have between three and seven chickens, an area of 1.5m x 1.5m (5ft x 5ft) is ideal. For a larger flock, increase the size to 2m x 2m (6½ft x 6½ft). You are aiming to make a U-shaped composting bay. The open side allows easy access for you and the chickens.

2. Nail two corner posts to either end of a length of scrap wood, then nail one length of wood to each post to create a U shape. Place a heavy stone on the outer edge of the two side boards to prevent them splaying out.

3. Cover any grass with a triple layer of cardboard to prevent it growing through. Over time the grass will naturally die off.

4. Now begin adding compost ingredients to the middle of the structure, a bucket load at a time and no more than 3–4 per day.

Every couple of weeks, turn over the material using a pitchfork then level it out to form a flat surface. This will expose bugs, seeds, weed sprouts, and plant material for the chickens to eat.

5. Continue this process until the pile starts building in size. At this point, turn over just the top 30cm (12in). You should see a thriving colony of worms underneath this layer.

6. To collect compost for mulching, scrape off the top 15–20cm (6–8in) of material, put it to one side and dig out as much compost as you need. If you have excess compost put in a "holding pile" elsewhere.

7. Finally, place the material that was pushed to one side back over the area and repeat the whole process.

TIP

YOU CAN ALSO USE A PHYSICAL CORNER (SUCH AS A WALL) AND JUST ADD ONE EXTRA BOARD FOR THE FINAL SIDE TO CREATE A BAY.

Watching chickens in their element always amazes me – it's great to see them have so much fun exploring all the material in the pile.

MULTI-STAGE METHOD

With at least five birds and a chicken run, you can create a "production-line" that will produce a steady supply of compost.

Producing fantastic mineral- and microbe-rich chicken compost for immediate use on the garden, this method is suitable for larger spaces. You will need at least five chickens for the smallest system; the example outlined on this page is perfect for 10 to 12 chickens. Using the same composting ingredients as the deep-mulch method (see previous page), this technique may take a little more time but you are guaranteed a consistent supply of compost throughout the year.

HOW IT WORKS

Starting with the pile of raw composting ingredients, you turn it regularly then move it on to the next stage – but only after an absolute minimum of 10 days. The chickens will also scratch and peck at the material, but it is essential to turn the heap over to incorporate oxygen and unearth weed sprouts and insects for the chickens to eat. By the end of the line you will have fully broken-down compost.

1. Deposit composting materials (approximately half green and half brown) into a pile at Stage 1. Every five days turn and then rake the pile back up into a mound. Continue this routine, building the pile up until it is at least 75cm x 75cm (30in x 30in) in size.

2. Use a pitchfork to move the pile to Stage 2 and start a new pile with fresh material at Stage 1. Every five days turn and rake both piles back up into mounds. Once the new pile at Stage 1 has reached 75cm x 75cm (30in x 30in), move it to Stage 2 and move that pile along to Stage 3. This is a continuous process so when each pile reaches the required size, you move it on to the next stage.

3. Continue to add material to the pile at Stage 1, and always turn and mound the piles at each of the stages in the same session every five days.

4. Depending on how quickly new piles build up, you should have beautiful fluffy compost by Stage 4 or 5 that is ready for use. If you have too much material, make each pile bigger rather than adding more stages.

5. Use the finished compost right away. If that isn't possible, create a holding pile and cover it with cardboard to keep the rain off.

TIP

MAKE TURNING THE COMPOST HEAPS PART OF YOUR CHICKEN-FEEDING ROUTINE AND KEEP A PITCHFORK HANDY.

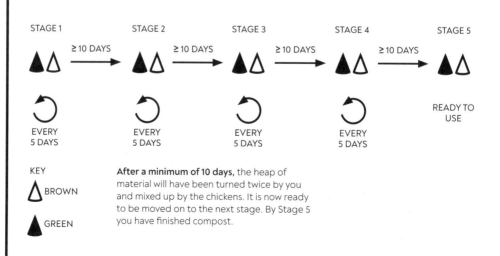

STAGE 1	STAGE 2	STAGE 3	STAGE 4	STAGE 5
≥ 10 DAYS	≥ 10 DAYS	≥ 10 DAYS	≥ 10 DAYS	
EVERY 5 DAYS	EVERY 5 DAYS	EVERY 5 DAYS	EVERY 5 DAYS	READY TO USE

KEY
△ BROWN
▲ GREEN

After a minimum of 10 days, the heap of material will have been turned twice by you and mixed up by the chickens. It is now ready to be moved on to the next stage. By Stage 5 you have finished compost.

NOTE

In the UK, disease-prevention controls prohibit the feeding of kitchen scraps to chickens. The solution is to process your vegetables outside so you can safely feed the chickens vegetable tops and peelings before you take your harvest indoors.

HOW MUCH COMPOST?

For a simple backyard system with 10 to 12 chickens and a good external source of supplementary materials, you should expect at least 5m³ (176ft³) of compost a year. Following no-dig principles, this volume is sufficient for spreading a 5cm (2in) layer of mulch over 25 raised beds, each measuring 3m x 1.2m (10ft x 4ft), on an annual basis.

Our chickens are part of the family. We have eight and in return for food, bedding, and lots of adventure they provide us with delicious eggs and fantastic compost for the garden.

HOT COMPOSTING

GREAT COMPOST IN FOUR TO SIX WEEKS

_____

When you're creating a new growing area from scratch and need compost as soon as possible – and your garden isn't suitable for keeping chickens – hot composting is a great solution.

HOW TO MAKE HOT COMPOST

Hot composting results in fantastic homemade compost that is
ideal for sowing, transplanting, and mulching.

This method will produce enough compost to mulch approximately eight to ten 1.2m x 3m (4ft x 10ft) raised beds – and there are other benefits, too. Hot composting (as opposed to the cold method) generates more heat, which not only speeds up the decomposition process but also also kills weed seeds as well as the bacteria and fungi that cause diseases, such as powdery mildew. The only downside is that a large quantity of compostable material is needed right at the beginning, so when using this method always plan to source everything upfront.

Materials and tools

- 1.5m x 1.5m (5ft x 5ft) square of cardboard
- Fork
- 50/50 mix of enough green and brown compostable material to make a pile at least 1m³ (3ft³) in volume
- Spadeful of ready-made compost or well-rotted woodchip as an activator
- 2m x 2m (6ft x 6ft) piece of hessian or breathable material for insulation
- Stones or bricks
- Compost thermometer

Note: avoid large woody prunings and chop material thoroughly before adding to the pile. You could use a wheelbarrow and shears.

1. Set aside a suitable piece of ground where you can build the compost heap. You'll need a space of at least 2m x 2m (6ft x 6ft). First cut any grass then place the cardboard layer on the ground.
2. Begin piling the compost materials in the centre, mixing greens and browns with a fork as you go. Aim to create a tall mound of material that is at least 1.2m (4ft) wide at the base and 80cm (32in) tall, and add the spadeful of compost/woodchip halfway through the process.
3. Soak the pile until you see water running out from underneath, then cover it with hessian. Put stones or bricks on top to prevent the hessian blowing off.
4. Push the thermometer through the hessian into the heart of the mound to monitor the internal temperature. Return the following day to check it. Ideally, the pile should reach a temperature of 43°–65°C (109°–149°F).

Continue monitoring the temperature daily, use your fork to turn the pile when needed, and then cover it over and replace the thermometer. After four to six weeks you should have a pile of rich, earthy-smelling compost that feels light and airy. Let it sit for a further week, then use.

TIP

FOR SPEEDIER DECOMPOSITION, USE A WATERING CAN WITH A ROSE TO APPLY 2ML (⅓TSP) OF LAB (SEE PP139–141) DILUTED WITH 1 LITRE (2 PINTS) OF WATER TWO DAYS AFTER CREATING THE PILE.

TROUBLESHOOTING

- **Smelly pile** If the problem persists for more than two days there is too much nitrogen (green material) so add more brown material, such as torn-up cardboard or a little sawdust.
- **Pile is too hot** If the temperature rises above 65°C (149°F), cool the heap down by moving material from the middle (the core) to the outside or you risk killing beneficial microbes. If the temperature falls below 43°C (109°F), turning the pile will introduce more oxygen to help it reheat.
- **Pile isn't warm enough** Mix in more nitrogen-rich greens and ensure the pile is as moist as a wrung-out sponge. Also check you've made the pile big enough. Used coffee grounds are excellent for boosting nitrogen levels.
- **Too wet** Cover the pile with tarpaulin so it doesn't become saturated during prolonged rainfall. Remove it once drier weather arrives.

SOURCING EXTRA MATERIALS

HELP IS AT HAND

Sometimes you might need to source extra materials so you can generate enough compost. Set up a simple collection system and pick up free, compostable ingredients from neighbours, friends, and family.

" "

WHEN IT COMES TO COMPOSTABLE MATERIALS, ONE PERSON'S TRASH CAN BE A GARDENER'S TREASURE.

Apart from available space, access to sufficient quantities of compostable material is the only factor that will limit the amount of compost home growers can produce. An average size 1m x 1m (3ft x 3ft) bin is a hungry beast that will take a long time to fill using just kitchen and garden waste and an individual household is very unlikely to generate enough material. Fortunately, as gardeners we can call on our greatest asset – neighbours – to help us fill up our compost bins more quickly.

CREATE A WISH LIST

Remembering that good compost needs a mix of green and brown materials (see p52), draw up a list of ingredients that neighbours could feasibly provide given your location (rural, urban, or suburban). Try not to overwhelm people with too many options and restrict your list to three green and three brown ingredients. Write the list down on a piece of card and make another four or five copies to distribute.

RECRUITMENT

Once you've made your cards, approach neighbours as well as any friends or family living nearby and explain that you're collecting ingredients to increase your compost capacity and need extra material. Make sure you set up a system that is straightforward and requires minimal effort on their part. For example, supply a bucket and ask neighbours to leave it out for collection on a specific day every week. You then collect the bucket, empty the contents

on the compost bin, then return it cleaned to the same spot a day or so later. A simple routine is the best guarantee of success.

This method works best in rural and suburban areas where buckets can be placed outside the property and neighbours don't have to be at home. For urban areas, arrange a convenient time in advance for both collection and return.

COLLECTION CONTAINERS

The ideal container for collecting compostable ingredients is a 10- or 20-litre (2.2 or 4.4 gallon) standard bucket with a handle for easy carrying. Make sure it also has a lid to keep contents and smells in and foraging creatures out. Buckets are inexpensive, widely available from hardware stores, and easily rinsed out with a hose. You can also invest in galvanized steel buckets for extra durability and protection.

RETURNING THE FAVOUR

Perhaps the most crucial element when sourcing materials from neighbours is to show your appreciation for their efforts. Ideally, share some of your harvests with them and be generous with homegrown flowers or homemade preserves. In return for such thoughtful gifts you are more likely to receive consistent supplies of great composting material for the long term.

Picking up just one extra bucket of material a week will result in noticeably more compost by the end of the growing season.

CHOP AND DROP

A GREAT ALTERNATIVE TO COMPOSTING

A quick and easy technique, chop and drop promotes a fantastic, healthy, microbe-rich soil. Rather than moving organic material to a compost bin, you can process it right there and then.

When a plant dies or sheds material, this organic matter falls on the ground, breaks down, and releases its nutrients back into the earth. Chop and drop mimics nature's rhythm and is an effective way of recycling nutrients. By processing the material in one place, you return goodness and organic matter directly to the soil.

CHOP AND DROP METHOD

Simply remove any excess plant material, chop it up, and spread it over the same piece of ground the plants were growing in. For example, when harvesting a patch of summer cabbages you remove the outer leaves to leave a clean head of cabbage. Rather than adding these outer leaves to the compost, chop them up finely and lightly spread them over the patch that you've just cleared.

You can apply chop and drop to any non-diseased plant material, as well as weeds that haven't set seed, and it can be done at any time of year. I tend to use chop and drop from summer onwards when second plantings replace the spring sowings.

When you've collected the material – I like to put it in a wheelbarrow – the only tool you need is a sharp pair of shears. Chop the material into the smallest possible pieces (about 1cm/⅓in) because the smaller the size, the quicker it breaks down. Also, organic matter tends to decompose faster on the surface of the soil than if you add it to a half-full compost pile.

If possible, chop and drop on a warm sunny day to encourage the material to wilt and kickstart the decomposition process. Add light layers no thicker than 1.5cm (½in) – any deeper and you'll create a habitat for slugs. If you have any leftover processed material, spread it nearby or compost it.

CHOP, MOVE, AND DROP

Using this variation on the standard method, you "harvest" material from a different location (preferably nearby) and move it into the garden to chop up, and then drop on the cleared bed. Organic material, including nettles, comfrey, prunings from the herb bed, and grass clippings all work well. Nettles, in particular, are hugely underrated and and bring great benefits to the vegetable garden (see p196).

TIP

PERENNIALS ARE PERFECT FOR THE CHOP, MOVE, AND DROP TECHNIQUE. I OFTEN MULCH PERENNIALS, SUCH AS SOFT FRUIT, WITH COMFREY AND NETTLES.

Finely chop up plant material into 1cm (⅓in) pieces, using a sharp pair of shears.

Drop and spread the material over cleared ground. Here, I am returning radish, chard, and nasturtium leaves to the soil.

PREPARING FOR WINTER

PUTTING BEDS TO SLEEP

Whenever you harvest a vegetable, you are effectively removing nutrients from the soil. Therefore adding organic matter in autumn is a great way to boost soil health in time for spring while reducing winter weeds.

Autumn is the perfect time to put some goodness back into the soil and help prepare the ground for the next growing season. Whether beds are empty or still growing winter crops, I have outlined simple processes for you to follow so that your growing area maintains healthy soil, keeps weed-free, and is as productive as ever.

There are five major advantages to this approach:
- Frees you up to focus on planning during winter
- Replenishes soil nutrients
- Preserves soil structure
- Prevents weeds from growing
- Creates "planting-ready" beds for spring

IF WE LOOK AFTER THE SOIL, THE SOIL WILL LOOK AFTER OUR CROPS.

PUTTING BEDS TO SLEEP

When the growing season is over and the ground is clear, follow the steps below and aim to finish preparation by mid-December.

1. Clear the bed of any leftover plants that are not worth harvesting or saving for seed, such as bolted lettuce. Cut these down at soil level so you leave the roots in the ground to decompose, and pile the green material into a wheelbarrow. When removing weeds, dig them up roots and all, and put them straight into the compost bin.
2. Take a pair of shears and chop up the plant material in the wheelbarrow as finely as you can. When everything is in small pieces, spread a light covering – no thicker than 1cm (½in) – over the surface of the bed. If there is any material left over, either compost it or use it on a different bed.
3. Apply a layer of compost, between 2.5cm–5cm (1–2in) thick, over the chopped material. For an average-sized

(3m x 1.2m/10ft x 4ft) raised bed this will usually amount to between one and two wheelbarrow-loads of compost.
4. Now cover the bed to exclude light and prevent weeds from growing. Nothing is worse than starting a new growing season with beds full of weeds! Organic material, such as cardboard, is easy to source in abundance and can be placed on top and weighed down with stones and branches. I've also used old landscape fabric.

Once the bed has been covered, simply leave it alone all winter. You can then look forward to my favourite part removing the covering in spring to reveal beautiful, healthy soil that is just ready for sowing and growing.

TIP

AN EASY WAY TO CHOP UP PLANT MATERIAL IS TO SPREAD IT ON THE GROUND AND RUN THE LAWNMOWER OVER IT.

TIP

ALWAYS GET
QUOTES FROM
DIFFERENT COMPOST
SUPPLIERS TO WORK
OUT THE MOST
AFFORDABLE
OPTION.

BEDS WITH WINTER VEGETABLES

Not all beds can be put to sleep because crops for harvesting over winter will still be in them. These tend to be slow growing and will be harvested over a period of months so the beds don't need much attention. I choose from one of two options to decide if and when to mulch these beds:

Option 1

For beds that will be clear by late winter, I hold off and mulch the soil once all the vegetables have been harvested but don't bother covering the bed. Instead, I keep on top of any emerging weeds by hitting them early using an oscillating hoe. If a bed becomes free from early to mid-winter, then I mulch and cover as described on the previous page.

Option 2

It isn't essential to mulch beds with long-term winter crops because the plants won't grow much during the darkest months. I make an exception for overwintering kale. In mid-winter, I apply a 2.5–5cm (1–2in) layer of compost around the stems so I can pick the edible flower shoots in spring.

BEDS UNDER COVER

In polytunnels, beds are sheltered from the rain so the soil has a tendency to dry out. If crops are still growing, mulch with compost and make sure you water regularly. Where beds under cover are empty and looking dry in autumn, I simply give them a good soak. This supplies the beneficial microbes with the moisture they need and stops the soil from turning to dust. After watering, I prepare the bed for winter, using the chop and drop technique (see p66), then mulch with compost.

Covering the beds is optional, but I like to put down a layer of newspaper to help prevent evaporation and keep the soil moist.

NOT ENOUGH COMPOST?

When compost supplies are running low and you don't have enough to mulch your beds, consider the following alternatives.

Manure

Horse and/or cow manure is a great alternative to compost but it must be very well rotted, not fresh. Source it from neighbouring farms or smallholdings but always check what the animals were fed before you buy (see opposite). Finding animal manure suppliers in urban areas might be a struggle, so think about setting up a community compost scheme (see p204).

Bulk compost

This short-term solution is much cheaper than purchasing individual bags of compost, which come in non-renewable plastic. There are bulk compost suppliers nationwide, with most offering delivery as long as you order a tonne or more. Consider splitting the cost of a bulk delivery with other gardeners to enjoy great-quality compost at a discount. Or if you have a large garden, and space for storage, arrange a bulk delivery of green waste from your local council, as I have done in the past.

Increase production

The obvious long-term solution is to produce more homemade compost. As a rule of thumb, a well-filled 1m³ (3ft³) bin will yield enough compost to mulch between four and five standard-sized (3m x1.2m/10ft x 4ft) raised beds depending on how thickly you spread it. Use this as a guide to work out how many bins you might need (see pp52–57 for advice). Material in hot bins tends to shrink less, giving you a greater volume of compost (see p62). It's something to bear in mind when working out how many beds you can mulch per bin-load of homemade compost.

Ensure the soil in your beds is moist right through winter and into early spring. Check them every couple of weeks, even if mulched with compost or newspaper.

WARNING

In recent years many gardeners unwittingly used manure laced with aminopyralid – a herbicide – with disastrous results. Crops grown for animal forage are often sprayed, eaten by livestock and the herbicides then pass into their manure, which becomes contaminated. When spread on the soil, it can severely stunt the development of many plants. Unless you know your supplier follows organic principles, always ask what their animals have been fed.

SEED STARTING
AND TRANSPLANTING

How to start off seeds in modules, transplant, sow direct, and care for seedlings

ORGANIZING SEEDS

SMART WAYS TO STORE

Some gardeners (me included) are seed hoarders but this sometimes makes looking for a specific packet difficult. Organizing my own seeds has been a small but significant step to improved efficiency.

STORE YOUR SEEDS IN A COOL DARK PLACE TO MAINTAIN GOOD VIABILITY.

STORAGE SYSTEMS

I'd like to share three low- to medium-cost seed storage ideas to help you keep track of your assorted packets. Once seeds have been organized, it's so much easier to identify any gaps that need filling when it's time to put in your seed order.

Takeaway boxes

Small plastic boxes for takeaway food make excellent airtight containers to store seeds in. Depending on how many crops you grow, either use one box per vegetable, or one per group of vegetables and label the box as soon as you've filled it. The downside of this method is that the boxes take up a fair amount of space. Choose one of the other options if your storage is limited.

Shoebox

Adding individual compartments to shoeboxes makes them low-cost seed organizers. I make my own dividers for free from cardboard and fix them inside with tape. This task can be a little fiddly but I find using wide parcel tape helps. I usually have one group of seeds per section, such as brassicas, salads, or root vegetables. The shoeboxes are also deep enough for the packets to stand up so you can flick through easily and pick out what you need. Alternatively, attach a label to each compartment. For larger shoeboxes, create compartments by cutting the tops off drinks cartons and slotting in their bases.

Photo organizer

If your gardening budget allows, the best seed-storage solution is a photo organizer with several different labelled compartments. You can carry it around in one hand without spilling seed packets, and it takes up very little storage space. I learnt of this amazing method from Tanya Anderson, author of *A Woman's Garden*, and although upfront investment is required, this is probably the only seed organizer you'll ever need!

ANNUAL SEED DECLUTTER

At the end of each growing season, try to get into the habit of laying out all your seeds on a table so you can sort through them. Set aside seeds past or close to their "sow by" date, half-empty packets, and seeds you've inadvertently bought too many of. For the next growing season, prioritize the seeds that are close to or have just passed their sow by date. These should be sown first then followed by those in half-empty packets. Donate those seeds you've got in abundance to new gardeners or take them to community seed swaps to trade for crops you're low on. Once you've decluttered your collection and are up to date, you will be more confident of buying what you need when it's time to put in your seed order.

My seed collection is stored in boxes, including two lovely red ones that I was given on my birthday.

TIP

AIM TO ORDER YOUR
SEEDS BEFORE
CHRISTMAS. MANY
SEED MERCHANTS
CAN RUN LOW
ON CERTAIN
VEGETABLES AND
OTHERS MAY SELL
OUT COMPLETELY.

PROPAGATION SETUP

SOWING AND POTTING

A dedicated area for sowing seeds ensures a positive start to a new growing season. Below, I've created a list of essentials for the most productive and efficient setup, from good ventilation to shelving and key tools.

TIP

KEEP A GARDEN PLAN (SEE PP160–163), PREFERABLY LAMINATED, NEXT TO YOUR PROPAGATION AREA SO YOU CAN SEE AT A GLANCE WHAT NEEDS SOWING AND WHEN.

A propagation setup involves two core areas: one for potting up seedlings and another for storing them. A three-sided potting tray is ideal for the first and you can make your own from scrap wood or board. Secondly, when you've filled seed trays and pots, stacking them on a shelving unit is practical and also saves space. The checklist below sets out eight essentials for a productive seed-propagation area.

Good light and airflow
If you have a polytunnel or a greenhouse, the ideal spot for the propagating area is south-facing near the entrance for adequate light and good airflow. If you don't have space under cover, consider investing in a mini-greenhouse or a cold frame. Seedlings can also be raised on a sunny windowsill provided you rotate the trays or pots 180 degrees daily and open the window regularly.

Access to water
Water is vital for thirsty seedlings so make sure that a supply is close at hand. Set up an extension to your garden hose or keep full watering cans nearby if your growing area isn't close to the house.

A sturdy bench and tray
Make sure your bench is stable then build or buy a small potting tray so you can fill modules and pots with compost without wasting or spilling it. There are many products online from low-cost plastic to wood or durable galvanized steel.

Shelving
Good airflow under pots is important to encourage a strong root system and I'll explain later why wire mesh is the perfect shelving material (see p82). I invested in a wide mini-greenhouse for the polytunnel because it takes up very little floor space in comparison to the large numbers of seed trays and pots you can store on the shelves.

Compost and pots
For convenience, I keep my pots, modules, and seed trays on a shelf directly under the potting bench but I don't think it's necessary to wash them before sowing. Also, I always have a bag or bucket of compost on the floor by the bench that's ready to use at a moment's notice. Keeping a cover over this small batch will prevent the compost drying out.

Tools
I use three principal tools for seed sowing and seedling care: i) a small pair of secateurs for thinning seedlings and cutting down yogurt pots into seed labels, ii) a small watering can for watering seeds and seedlings, iii) a pencil – the pointed end is useful for separating small seedlings, such as lettuce and tomatoes, when potting them on.

Labels
The need to label what you sow is obvious. I keep a plant pot filled with labels, marker pens, and pencils on the bench.

Potting trays (*left*) and the wire mesh shelves of a mini-greenhouse (*below*) are ideal for seed propagation and seedling care.

Protection

Under cover seedlings are still susceptible to frosts on cold nights so I keep some horticultural fleece in the propagation area to drape over the shelving unit if low temperatures are forecast. An alternative is to use an old bedsheet.

SOWING IN MODULES

START SEEDS UNDER COVER

For an efficient and productive vegetable garden, I recommend sowing seeds in modules under cover. You can get ahead when it's not warm enough to sow direct and have seedlings ready to plant when a previous crop is harvested.

> " "
>
> WHEN SOWING SEEDS, IT'S ESSENTIAL THEY DON'T DRY OUT, BUT DON'T GO TO THE OTHER EXTREME AND SATURATE THEM.

MODULE TRAYS

Until fairly recently, only flimsy plastic seed trays were available to gardeners and the individual cells would split after just a couple of seasons' use. Owing to increased demand and environmental awareness, home growers now have access to the high-quality module trays only previously available to the horticulture industry – a game-changer for starting seeds under cover. These rigid trays, often made from recycled plastic, are more expensive but they should last at least 15 years, accommodate more seeds, and use less compost than previous models. They also have a finger-sized hole at the base, which makes transplanting a breeze! Find links to recommended suppliers in the Resources section (p216). Below are the four types of propagation tray I use on a regular basis:

- **Small-celled** (30mm/1¼in) Perfect for smaller seeds such as lettuce, fennel and spinach.
- **Medium-celled** (42mm/1½in) My favourite size, very versatile, and the one I use most often. Perfect for brassicas, beetroot, salads, herbs and peas. Also fantastic for starting off annual flowers such as cosmos and calendula.
- **Large-celled** (75mm/3in plus) Fantastic for potting on brassicas and herb cuttings and much easier to move around than several individual pots. Only recommended if you have space available under cover. Also works well for dwarf beans.
- **Deep-celled** (40–50mm/1½–2in) Brilliant for starting off beans, especially those with a tap-root tendency such as broad beans.

COMPOST TYPES

I only ever use two types for any herb, fruit, flower, and vegetable I sow. The first is homemade compost that has been left to break down for longer than usual (at least 12 months) so any larger pieces of material have had time to decompose. The resulting compost has a finer texture that is much more suitable for sowing smaller seeds. I prefer using my own compost for sowing, but if supplies are running low I often mix two handfuls of homemade compost with a handful of garden soil. You might want to use this as your regular sowing mix on the basis that your seedlings will start out in some of the soil they will later be transplanted into.

Organic multi-purpose compost is my second choice but because it is currently available only in plastic bags I buy as little as possible. My great hope is that it will soon be available in plastic-free packaging.

MULTISOWING

Originally employed in large-scale vegetable production, this ingenious technique has only recently hit the home-growing mainstream – thanks to organic grower and no-dig authority, Charles Dowding. Multiple seedlings are sown together and allowed to grow on, rather than being thinned when they reach a certain size. Beetroot, for example, can be sown in multiples of 4–5 seedlings. When transplanted, the beetroot will mature at different rates so you harvest only the biggest from each clump at a time. This form of succession growing and planting is not only ideal for small-space gardens but it also saves time on larger plots. Compared to traditional direct sowing, multisowing is a quicker, less wasteful, and more efficient method. On the right is a chart I adapted from information on Charles Dowding's website listing vegetables suitable for multisowing plus the target seed number per module.

Plant companions

Charles Dowding once said that plants benefit from being multisown and then grown on together because they like being "with their friends". This sums up perfectly the importance of communities, which is how plants grow and thrive in nature (see pp20–23). For example, different types of trees growing together in rural areas tend to live longer, healthier lives than single trees in urban settings.

CROP	SEEDS PER MODULE
Beetroot	4–5
Chard (salad leaf)	3–4
Chard (for cooking)	1–2
Kale (salad leaf)	2–3
Leek	3–4
Onion (for cooking)	4–5
Onion (salad)	6–7
Peas (pods)	2–4
Peas (shoots)	3–4
Salad crops (spinach, lettuce, rocket etc)	2–3
Swede (early crops)	2–3
Radish	5–7
Turnip	3–4

Multisowing crops, such as turnips (*above*), beetroot (*top right*), and sweet peas (*bottom right*) saves time.

HOW TO SOW IN MODULES

All you need is a potting bench, module tray, compost, water, and, of course, seeds!

1. Fill a module tray with compost, preferably on a potting bench or other flat surface.

2. Firm the compost with your hand so the surface is level.

3. Water well and leave for 5 minutes to allow the compost to become thoroughly moist with no air pockets.

4. Make a hole with your finger in each cell. Don't worry if the depth isn't accurate. To speed things up, I use three fingers of one hand to make multiple seed holes at the same time.

5. Take your seeds (here I'm sowing peas) and drop one into a hole. Don't worry if an extra seed falls in. Repeat until you've filled the tray.

6. Add a large handful of compost to the middle of the tray and spread it out over the cells to cover the seeds, pressing down slightly.

7. Label the tray and give it another water.

TIP

FOR A DURABLE ALTERNATIVE TO CARDBOARD, MEASURE AND CUT SECTIONS OF WOODEN BOARD TO ACT AS LONG-TERM TRAY COVERS.

CONSERVING MOISTURE

Compost drying out is often the cause of poor germination rates. Seeds must be kept moist at this vital stage so need frequent watering. This can be time-consuming so to conserve moisture, I cover the whole seed tray with a layer of cardboard or a few layers of newspaper straight after watering. You don't need to water as often, even in very warm weather, because this method greatly reduces evaporation. Here's what to do:

1. Cut out a piece of cardboard slightly larger than the size of the module tray, or place 5–7 sheets of newspaper over the tray.

2. Weigh down the four corners to anchor the cover, using pieces of wood or stones.

3. After 3–4 days lift the cover to check moisture levels. If the top 1cm (½in) has dried out, water the compost surface and re-cover (unless there are signs of growth).

4. As soon as you see any green shoots, remove the cardboard or newspaper and put it in the compost bin.

Place small stones on top of cardboard tray covers to stop them being blown off by a gust of wind.

MODULE-SOWN SEEDLING CARE

TLC FOR TINY PLANTS

When sown in modules and pots, thirsty seedlings require a steady supply of water. Good air circulation, especially around the base of the container, is also necessary to produce healthy plants.

Seedlings grown under cover can very easily become stressed owing to erratic watering, while overcrowding will leave them vulnerable to disease. At this crucial stage in their development, correct watering and spacing between seedlings are vital.

WATERING MODULE-SOWN SEEDLINGS

One of the easiest ways to water seedlings in modules is to dip the tray or pots in a large shallow container filled with about 2.5cm (1in) of water. Leave the containers for 15-20 minutes so the water can work its way right up through compost. Once the surface is moist, put the tray or pot back onto the shelf.

When watering trays and pots from above, the water tends to run over the surface, not down through the compost. This is inevitable when the compost is very dry and has shrunk away from the sides of the pot, allowing water to drain straight out of the bottom. Gentle overhead watering is a good idea when seedlings have not dried out and just need a top-up. However, watering from the base encourages the roots to grow downwards, creating a stronger plant.

AIR PRUNING

Wire-mesh shelves are ideal for pots and trays of seedlings grown under cover because they allow air to circulate freely around the plants. When a seedling's root reaches the base of a pot standing on wire mesh, the air will have a drying effect. This process is called "air pruning" because drying out restricts the growth of the main root. As with any other plant, root pruning

encourages the production of many smaller roots and this increased root surface area allows the seedling to take up additional moisture and nutrients from the compost. Given this head start, seedlings will be healthier and more resilient once transplanted.

DAMPING OFF

Good ventilation is also vital for seedlings sown undercover to prevent damping off. This fungal disease, which causes seedlings to flop and eventually die, tends to take hold when combined with two other factors – overcrowding and overwatering. Sowing thinly, following the watering guidance on this page, and setting pots and trays on wire mesh with space between them will all help to keep this disease at bay. I set up a mini-greenhouse inside the polytunnel to act as a low-cost mesh-shelving unit for my seedlings and have had great results.

> **THE STRONGER THE ROOT SYSTEM, THE HEALTHIER THE PLANT.**

Giving seedlings a top up of water (*top left*), an example of a healthy root system that has been air pruned (*top right*) and setting down a tray of spinach seedlings to soak up water from the base (*right*).

TRANSPLANTING TIPS

SETTLING SEEDLINGS INTO THE SOIL

For me, transplanting seedlings is one of the most satisfying gardening tasks. After many years, I decided to create my own checklist to ensure seedlings get the best possible start in life.

TIP

WHY NOT HAVE A DEDICATED SPACE IN YOUR POLYTUNNEL OR SHED FOR SOWING AND TRANSPLANTING TOOLS SO THEY ARE ALL IN ONE PLACE?

TRANSPLANTING CHECKLIST

Preparation is key to success so take a moment to run through the list below before you rush to plant out. My checklist is set out in the form of questions. Only when I can answer "yes" to all five questions, is it time to transplant.

Is it the right time?

I like to transplant seedlings when they have 4-5 true leaves – these usually appear after the first 2 leaves. I also like to check the weather forecast for storms or late frosts. The last thing I want is for my seedlings to be put under stress.

Is the ground moist?

After a dry spell, I always soak the transplanting area. Do this around an hour before you are ready to plant so the water can soak down into the soil to be taken up by the roots. Moist ground is also much easier to make planting holes in than dry soil.

Have the seedlings been pre-soaked?

It's a good idea to water your seedlings well before transplanting, preferably by standing the trays or pots in water (see p82). The seedlings will slip out easily and the moisture will help to keep the fragile root ball intact.

Do I have the right tools?

Although transplanting doesn't require much kit, I always make sure I have everything I need with me. Breaking off to fetch something I've forgotten is not an efficient use of time!

Have I double-checked my planting plan?

It's easy to plant seedlings in the wrong place but having spent time drawing up a planting plan, I always like to check it beforehand (see pp160–163). Mistakes don't cause big problems on the whole but I prefer to stick with the plan and avoid confusion.

TRANSPLANTING TOOLS

My favourite tool for transplanting small to medium-sized seedlings is the blunted end of a broken wooden spade handle. You might also have a favourite implement or prefer to use a small trowel to make holes in the soil. Other essentials for transplanting are a stringline for sowing in rows, plant labels, a pencil, and a full watering can.

TRANSPLANTING DEPTH

If my seedlings are looking a little leggy, I transplant them below the soil level so the first leaf is just above the surface. This helps to encourage a strong stem and root system and will work with all young vegetable plants except legumes. After transplanting, I make sure I've labelled the variety and give the seedlings a final water to welcome them into their new home.

Transplanting leek seedlings raised in a seed bed by dropping them into their final positions. Watering will settle soil around the roots.

DIRECT SOWING

IN SEEDBEDS AND DRILLS

Sowing in modules is great for succession planting and extending the season, however sowing direct is my go-to method for carrots and parsnips, which don't respond well to transplanting, and I always use it for salad crops.

I ALWAYS ENJOY THE PROCESS OF CREATING A TILTH BECAUSE I TAKE PRIDE IN HAVING IMMACULATE BEDS TO SOW SEEDS IN.

Sowing direct is less time-consuming than sowing in modules and then transplanting, although you will need to thin seedlings.

DO YOU NEED A TILTH?
Before sowing direct, traditional wisdom dictates that you create a "tilth" by carefully raking over the surface of the soil to remove any stones and large clumps of earth.
The tilth – the fine, crumbly surface layer – makes the ground easier to work as well as looking attractive. However, this process isn't essential and seeds will still germinate and grow well in soil that hasn't been raked over several times. If your soil is particularly coarse and creating a tilth will be very time

consuming, first make a drill (see below) and instead of pushing the soil back over it, cover the trench with sieved compost. Give this row plenty of water and use the plank method overleaf to help retain moisture.

SPACING DRILLS
When creating multiple drills in the same bed or piece of ground for direct sowing, spacing is key. Ensure there is enough space between each row for a hoe so you can keep on top of weeds as the seedlings develop. As long as the gaps are slightly wider than the head of my hoe, weed management is easy.

I tend to start off crops I use a lot of, such as brassicas and leeks, by sowing direct into their own dedicated seedbed.

HOW TO SOW DIRECT

Create a basic seed drill using a rake and line of string to sow direct.

1. Make a simple stringline measuring tool. Find two sticks, roughly 20cm (8in) long plus a length of string that's about 10cm (4in) longer than the width across your widest raised bed.
2. Insert one stick at either side of the bed and wind, then secure the string around each until you have a taut line.
3. Having created a perfectly straight guide, run a rake handle along the stringline to make a drill.

4. Sow seeds at the recommended spacing. If, like me, you sow too many you can thin them out once the seedlings are around 2.5cm (1in) tall (see overleaf).
5. Cover the seeds using the displaced soil and water thoroughly.
6. Remove the stringline but place two smaller sticks in the same position to serve as "row reminders" and then make a label so you don't forget what you've sown.

KEEPING SEEDLINGS MOIST

Ensure you keep all direct-sown seeds well watered to help them germinate successfully but try not to saturate them! As with seeds sown in modules, it is vital that direct-sown seeds don't dry out. A dry soil during the germination process will result in erratic or even failed germination, especially when sowing parsnips and carrots. The seeds of these two vegetables are very moisture-sensitive and are highly susceptible to failure if the ground dries out during this vital stage. Water seeds well and then adopt the plank method below to conserve moisture.

The plank method

Once the rows have been watered after sowing, I like to use the "plank method", pioneered by permaculture founder Bill Mollison (see pp16–19), to reduce evaporation and increase the germination rates of seeds sown in beds. Source planks slightly narrower than your bed (such as pallet planks or scaffold boards) and gently lay them directly over the row. The "row reminder" sticks (see step 6 on the previous page) will act as a guide, helping you lay down the planks correctly so you can see where the seeds were sown.

The plank is an excellent soil moisture-retention device that saves time by reducing the frequency of watering, but you should still be vigilant. On warm days lift the planks to check whether the ground is looking dry and water as necessary, then a few days after sowing, lift the plank daily to check for any green shoots. As soon as seedlings emerge, remove the plank and water the row well.

Planks also offer multiple benefits by acting as perfect slug traps. Check beneath the planks every morning and remove and dispose of any slugs hiding there. There will be fewer slugs around to munch your seedlings when they appear!

THINNING SEEDLINGS

Many people, myself included, are over-enthusiastic when sowing direct. When I've sown too many seeds and the resulting seedlings are crowded together, I use small garden scissors to remove the smaller and

I TRY TO SOW A FEW HOURS BEFORE RAIN IS FORECAST AND LET NATURE WATER THE SEEDS FOR ME.

Using the simple plank method gives me full confidence that the direct-sown seedlings will germinate successfully.

Garden "snips" with long thin blades are the perfect tool for getting in between delicate seedlings to thin them.

weaker seedlings to allow healthier ones to thrive. Simply snip off the seedling stem, preferably near the base. I love to use brassica and salad thinnings as a microgreen, otherwise I tend to leave the stems to dry out and break down on the surface. Never thin by pulling out seedlings because their fragile roots may be tangled up with those of their neighbours and you will accidentally uproot more than you intended.

WATER CARE

When seedlings are still in the early stage of development (before they have 6–7 true leaves) it is essential to water whenever the top 2cm (¾in) of soil is dry. After this, direct-sown seedlings are pretty resilient and need watering only every 3-4 days during dry weather. Mature plants often get enough moisture from rain, but if it hasn't rained for 7-10 days, give them a deep soaking.

HOW TO
GROW CROPS

Know when to start off, grow on, and harvest your favourite produce

GROWING ANNUALS

KEY CROPS OF THE KITCHEN GARDEN

Most homegrown vegetables are annuals and they offer a huge variety of flavours and textures as well as great yields. Harvesting them is a wonderful celebration of the changing seasons.

I AM SHARING THE TECHNIQUES I USE THAT SUIT ME BEST, BUT THE BEAUTY OF GARDENING IS THAT THERE IS ALWAYS SPACE FOR FLEXIBILITY.

Annual crops, as the name suggests, must be re-sown every year. They are all highly productive and if you are short on space you can maximize yields in small plots using techniques such as succession sowing (see p152). In the following pages you'll learn the essentials of sowing and growing annuals, as well as discover the methods I use that suit my site and situation. The information is not intended as a set of rules to follow, but as a rough guide that you adapt and build on in your own garden.

SIMPLIFYING THE PROCESS

Annuals do require more care and attention than perennial vegetables but much of the information about growing them has overcomplicated a simple process. This has motivated me to explore ways of simplifying how to grow them while ensuring my crops have the best chance of success.

BACK TO BASICS

Having covered sowing and transplanting (see pp78–89), it's important to now adapt these methods to individual crops. As soon as you have a solid understanding of how plants can be grown, it is easy to make the small adjustments that are required for each annual vegetable. Having given your crops the best possible start, other factors then come into play such as soil health, observation, biodiversity, and working with the seasons.

SOWING TIMES

In the growing profiles for each individual crop, the "sow under cover" and "sow direct" times err on the side of caution. In most cases, if you stick to these dates you will not need to worry about protecting crops from cold weather. If, however, you want to get ahead and can offer the protection of cloches or fleece, you can bring forward the sowing (and transplanting) dates of hardy and half-hardy crops by around 2 weeks if using fleece, and 3–4 weeks if using cloches. See p144 for more information on frost protection.

MASTER GROWING CHART

Overleaf is the chart I created to help me plan the growing season for my location. I also use it as a quick reference point to see what I can sow at any given period in the year. For example, if I know there will be a gap coming up in June, I can decide which crops can be started off in modules in May ready to fill that gap. To be clear, this chart is a personal resource that has been tailored to my regional climate with its strengths and limitations. Crops can be sown in other months, depending on where you live (see pp94–99 for more information).

There is something magical about harvesting an abundance of crops you've nurtured from seedlings; here, I'm adding freshly picked garden peas to my basket.

MASTER GROWING CHART

WHEN TO SOW, TRANSPLANT, AND HARVEST CROPS

With vital information about the growing season all in one place, this list is the most valuable resource I've created for my garden and I hope you'll find it as indispensable as I do.

The master growing chart (overleaf) is a simple yet effective way of setting out my preferred timings for growing any vegetable. I can see at a glance what to sow at any stage in the season, as well as choose appropriate plants to plug any gaps that emerge.

GROWING ZONES AND FROST DATES

A crucial element of gardening is to know which growing zone your region belongs to. These zones, also called hardiness zones, are categorized according to their average lowest annual temperature (see chart below).

ZONE	TEMPERATURE (°C)
1	-51.1 to -45.6
2	-45.6 to -40
3	-40 to -34.4
4	-34.4 to -28.9
5	-28.9 to -23.3
6	-23.3 to -17.8
7	-17.8 to -12.2
8	-12.2 to -6.7
9	-6.7 to -1.1
10	-1.1 to 4.4
11	4.4 to 10
12	10 to 15.6
13	15.6 to 21.1

The average lowest annual temperature in your region determines its growing zone, Crops that survive outdoors at this temperature are hardy.

Once you have this information, you can choose perennials and crops that will survive winter in your particular area. To find out more, go to Resources (see p216) where you'll find a website link. I garden in zone 8.

With your growing zone established, the next crucial piece of information is the average date of the first and last frosts in your area. Generally speaking, the period between these two dates represents a window for growing tender plants without the need for frost protection. My window is between mid-May and late-October and the information on the master growing chart reflects this. To find out your window consult gardeners in your area who are very familiar with local conditions, and remember to keep a close eye on the weather forecast.

MY MASTER GROWING CHART

Growers around the world garden in different zones with different climates. Some have a short window between frost dates, while others live in frost-free areas. The sowing information on the back of seed packets and in books can't possibly be specific to your location so it's best not to take it at face value. Experience and making detailed notes of weather conditions are the most reliable indicators of what is possible in your own garden in any growing season. The under cover and direct sowing dates given for all the crops listed in this chapter are taken from my own growing chart. They are intended as a guide and will be relevant to the majority of UK growers.

ALTHOUGH WE GARDEN AT THE MERCY OF THE WEATHER, THE MASTER GROWING CHART GIVES US THE BEST CHANCE OF A SUCCESSFUL GROWING SEASON.

YOUR BESPOKE CHART

Making your own master growing chart – specifically tailored to your garden – is the secret of successful growing. Use my list as a template then adapt the sowing, growing, and harvesting windows to your conditions and your personal preferences. If your last frost is in mid-April for example, you have an extra month upfront to start off crops. The master growing chart isn't set in stone: it will evolve as you continue your gardening journey.

Take a moment in early summer to check progress, bearing in mind when you sowed or planted out. If one of your crops took a while to get going, consider transplanting a couple of weeks later next year.

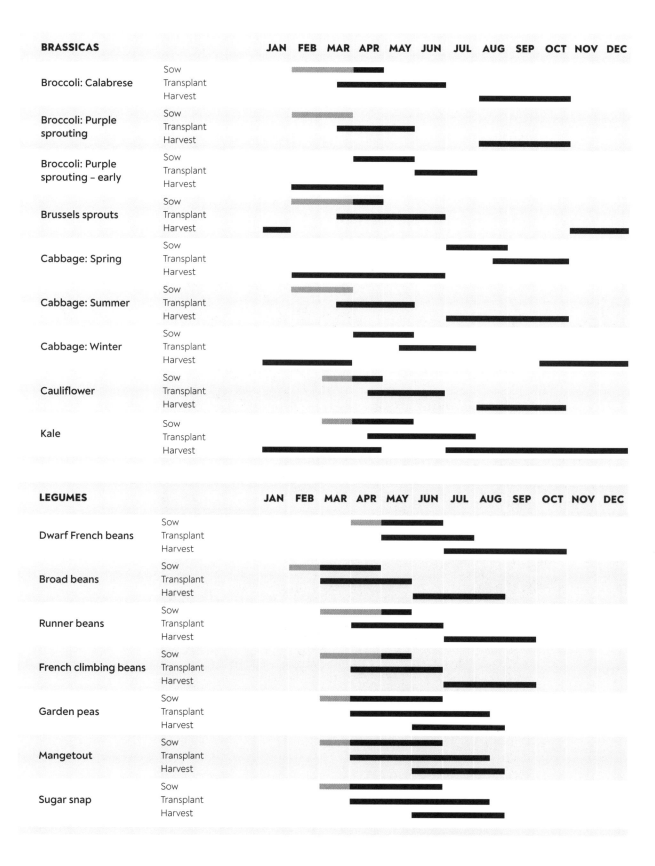

ROOTS AND STEMS

		JAN	FEB	MAR	APR	MAY	JUN	JUL	AUG	SEP	OCT	NOV	DEC
Beetroot	Sow												
	Transplant												
	Harvest												
Carrots	Sow												
	Transplant – N/A												
	Harvest												
Kohlrabi	Sow												
	Transplant												
	Harvest												
Parsnips	Sow												
	Transplant – N/A												
	Harvest												
Potatoes: Early	Sow												
	Transplant – N/A												
	Harvest												
Potatoes: Second	Sow												
	Transplant – N/A												
	Harvest												
Potatoes: Maincrop	Sow												
	Transplant – N/A												
	Harvest												
Radish	Sow												
	Transplant												
	Harvest												
Swede	Sow												
	Transplant												
	Harvest												
Turnips	Sow												
	Transplant												
	Harvest												
Winter radish	Sow												
	Transplant												
	Harvest												
Celery	Sow												
	Transplant												
	Harvest												
Celeriac	Sow												
	Transplant												
	Harvest												
Florence fennel	Sow												
	Transplant												
	Harvest												

KEY

Sow, transplant, harvest under cover

Sow, transplant, harvest outdoors

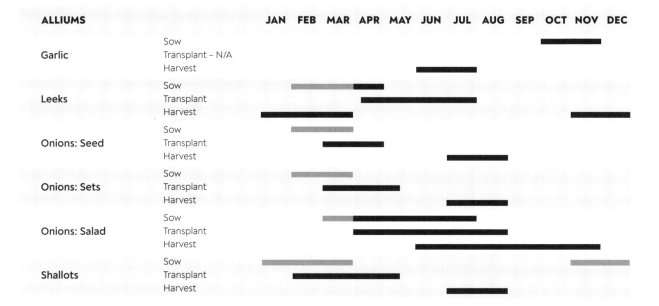

ALLIUMS

		JAN	FEB	MAR	APR	MAY	JUN	JUL	AUG	SEP	OCT	NOV	DEC

Garlic
Sow
Transplant – N/A
Harvest

Leeks
Sow
Transplant
Harvest

Onions: Seed
Sow
Transplant
Harvest

Onions: Sets
Sow
Transplant
Harvest

Onions: Salad
Sow
Transplant
Harvest

Shallots
Sow
Transplant
Harvest

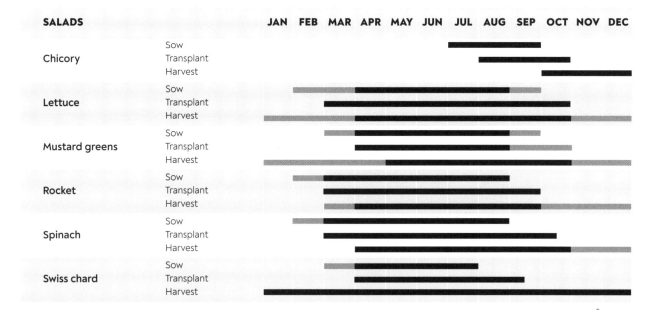

SALADS

		JAN	FEB	MAR	APR	MAY	JUN	JUL	AUG	SEP	OCT	NOV	DEC

Chicory
Sow
Transplant
Harvest

Lettuce
Sow
Transplant
Harvest

Mustard greens
Sow
Transplant
Harvest

Rocket
Sow
Transplant
Harvest

Spinach
Sow
Transplant
Harvest

Swiss chard
Sow
Transplant
Harvest

FRUITING VEGETABLES		JAN	FEB	MAR	APR	MAY	JUN	JUL	AUG	SEP	OCT	NOV	DEC
Aubergine	Sow		▓▓▓	▓▓									
	Transplant				■■	■■	■■						
	Harvest							■■	■■	■■	■		
Courgette and Summer squash	Sow			▓▓	▓▓	▓							
	Transplant			▓▓	▓▓	■■	■■						
	Harvest						■■	■■	■■	■■	■■		
Cucumbers	Sow			▓▓									
	Transplant				■■	■							
	Harvest							■■	■■	■■	■		
Peppers	Sow		▓▓▓	▓▓									
	Transplant				▓▓	■■	■■						
	Harvest							■■	■■	■■	■		
Pumpkins	Sow					▓▓							
	Transplant					■■							
	Harvest									■■	■■		
Winter squash	Sow				▓▓	▓							
	Transplant					■■							
	Harvest									■■	■■		
Sweetcorn	Sow					▓▓	■■						
	Transplant					■■	■■	■					
	Harvest								■■	■■			
Tomatoes	Sow			▓▓	▓								
	Transplant					▓▓	■■						
	Harvest							■■	■■	■■	■		

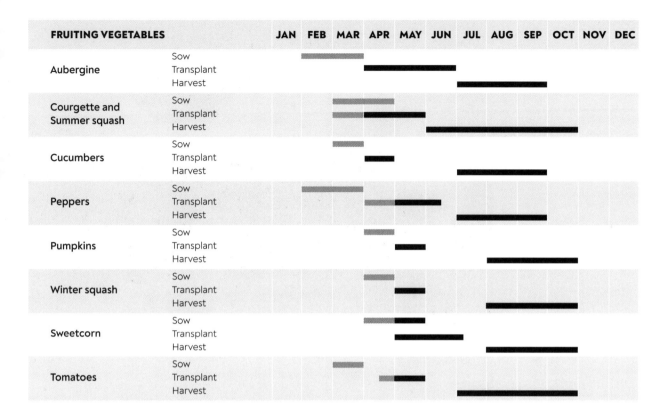

KEY

▓▓▓ Sow, transplant, harvest under cover

■■■ Sow, transplant, harvest outdoors

Beds filled with annual crops in full sun. Very soon the season of summer abundance will be well underway.

BRASSICAS

THE CABBAGE FAMILY

From this very broad group of vegetables, I've included only the large-stemmed varieties. Brassicas, especially cauliflower and Brussels sprouts, are hungry plants and seedlings need water and nutrients early on to guarantee great yields.

START OFF IN A SEEDBED

For earlier harvests and protection from attack by flea beetles, brassicas can be grown under cover in modules but I usually start by sowing in a seedbed in mid-spring. This allows me to grow a lot of seedlings in a small space and frees up under cover space. If you start off seedlings in smaller modules, then it's best to re-pot them into larger pots or modules once they have their first set of true leaves. Transplant module-grown seedlings once they have 4–5 true leaves.

TRANSPLANT DEPTHS

Brassica seedlings, especially if they haven't been thinned, can be a little leggy but this is easily remedied. Simply plant them deeply, burying the stems right up to the first set of true leaves to promote a strong plant.

FIRMING IN

Large-stemmed brassicas need to be firmly anchored in the ground to prevent them collapsing in gusts of wind or under the weight of the crop. After transplanting, I carefully firm in the roots with the flat of my foot. When any look like they're being buffeted about during windy weather, I insert a stick deeply into the ground and tie the plant to the stick for a little extra support.

PESTS

Flea beetles, cabbage white butterfly caterpillars, and pigeons can all inflict damage on brassica plants. See Pests (pp134–137) for control and solutions.

Brassica seedlings three weeks after being sown. The seedbed method is a great way to start off hundreds of plants in a small space.

SOWING AND TRANSPLANTING BRASSICAS

My preferred method for growing brassicas reduces time spent
on sowing, transplating, and watering.

1. Dedicate one end of a raised bed to brassicas and use the handle of a rake to make shallow drills 1–2cm (½–¾in) deep with a spacing of 15cm (6in) between rows.

2. Sow 1–2 seeds at 1cm (½in) intervals into the drill. You are aiming for 20–25 seedlings per 30cm (12in).

3. Cover the seeds with the displaced soil and water well.

4. If you are growing more than two varieties of brassica in one bed, use plant labels to mark where the variety changes.

5. Keep the rows of seedlings watered and thin them if you wish, although this isn't necessary (see pp88–89).

6. Once seedlings have developed 4–5 true leaves, gently lift from the soil and immediately transfer them to a bucket of water. This will maintain the seedlings' hydration levels and help you untangle the roots before transplanting.

7. Transplant seedlings into their final positions ensuring the soil level is just below the first set of true leaves. Water regularly for the first month if weather is dry.

Separate out individual plants from clumps of seedlings by holding the wet roots and gently shaking them to remove excess soil.

TIP

TO PREVENT FLEA BEETLE ATTACK, KEEP THE SEEDBED PERMANENTLY COVERED WITH A VERY FINE MESH.

BROCCOLI – CALABRESE

SOWING DEPTH
1–2CM (½–¾IN)

SOW UNDER COVER
**FROM 5–6 WEEKS
BEFORE LAST FROST**

SOW DIRECT
**FROM 2–3 WEEKS
BEFORE LAST FROST**

HARDINESS
HARDY

EFFORT
●●○○○○

Start off Either in a seedbed or under cover, sow 2–3 seeds per 7cm (2¾in) module/small pot filled with compost then thin to the strongest seedling.
Grow on Once seedlings have 4–5 true leaves, transplant into the ground and leave 35–40cm (13–16in) space between plants. Always place a generous handful of compost at the base of each planting hole. Once transplanted, firm around the seedling using your feet.
Harvest Calabrese is ready to harvest when the spears are nicely developed but haven't broken bud – from late summer to early autumn. Expect further cropping of smaller side shoots a month after the main harvest.

BROCCOLI – PURPLE SPROUTING

SOWING DEPTH
1–2CM (½–¾IN)

SOW UNDER COVER
**FROM 6–8 WEEKS
BEFORE LAST FROST**

SOW DIRECT
**FROM 2–3 WEEKS
BEFORE LAST FROST**

HARDINESS
VERY HARDY

EFFORT
●●○○○○

Start off As for calabrese. For early purple sprouting broccoli, sow 4–6 weeks later.
Grow on As for calabrese.
Harvest Harvest purple sprouting broccoli in the late summer and autumn of the year it was sown. Cut the spears before they turn into flower heads. Early purple sprouting broccoli is ready to harvest from early spring the following year.

BRUSSELS SPROUTS

SOWING DEPTH
1–2CM (½–¾IN)

SOW UNDER COVER
**5–6 WEEKS BEFORE
LAST FROST**

SOW DIRECT
**FROM 2–3 WEEKS
BEFORE LAST FROST**

HARDINESS
VERY HARDY

EFFORT
●●○○○○

Start off As for calabrese.
Grow on As for calabrese but leave just 30cm (12in) between plants when transplanting and firm in well. This will help to create well-formed individual sprouts on the stem. Later in the season, add support if needed by pushing a 80–90cm (32–36in) stake 30cm (12in) into the ground and then tying the stem loosely to it.
Harvest Harvest sprouts when firm to the touch, from late-autumn onwards, and pick those from the base of the plant first before working upwards.

CABBAGE – SPRING

SOWING DEPTH
1–2CM (½–¾IN)

SOW UNDER COVER
FROM EARLY SUMMER

SOW DIRECT
FROM EARLY SUMMER

HARDINESS
VERY HARDY

EFFORT
●●●○○○

Start off As for calabrese, but I would recommend sowing spring cabbage seed in modules rather than in a seedbed.
Grow on As for calabrese, but spacing between plants is dependent on cabbage variety. For smaller cabbages leave 30cm (12in); for larger increase space to 45cm (18in) between plants.
Harvest Spring cabbages may need netting to protect them from pigeons over the winter. They will begin to form heads from early spring onwards as the weather warms. Harvest as and when needed.

CABBAGE – SUMMER

Start off As for calabrese.
Grow on As for spring cabbage.
Harvest Harvest when heads are nice and firm, cutting the larger heads first to allow smaller ones to continue developing.

SOWING DEPTH
1–2CM (½–¾IN)

SOW UNDER COVER
**FROM 8 WEEKS
BEFORE LAST FROST**

SOW DIRECT
**FROM 2 WEEKS
BEFORE LAST FROST**

HARDINESS
HARDY

EFFORT
●●○○○

CABBAGE – WINTER

Start off As for calabrese.
Grow on As for spring cabbage.
Harvest As for summer cabbage.

SOWING DEPTH
1–2CM (½–¾IN)

SOW UNDER COVER
FROM MID-SPRING

SOW DIRECT
FROM MID-SPRING

HARDINESS
VERY HARDY

EFFORT
●●○○○

CAULIFLOWER

Start off As for calabrese.
Grow on Cauliflowers need very fertile soil so transplant into ground that has been well mulched with compost and/or well-rotted organic manure. Space plants 50–60cm (20–24in) apart; slightly wider for winter varieties. Watering is especially important when heads are forming so don't let the ground dry out at this stage.
Harvest Cut when heads are firm, from mid-summer onwards.

SOWING DEPTH
1–2CM (½–¾IN)

SOW UNDER COVER
**FROM 8-10 WEEKS
BEFORE LAST FROST**

SOW DIRECT
**FROM 2-3 WEEKS
BEFORE LAST FROST**

HARDINESS
HALF HARDY

EFFORT
●●●○○

KALE

Start off As for calabrese.
Grow on As for calabrese, but you can space plants slightly closer at around 30cm (12in).
Harvest Harvest a few leaves at a time from early summer onwards, as and when needed. Letting kale plants flower the following spring will yield an abundance of delicious sweet spears, similar to purple sprouting broccoli, to enjoy during the hungry gap (see p158).

SOWING DEPTH
1–2CM (½–¾IIN)

SOW UNDER COVER
**FROM 5-6 WEEKS
BEFORE LAST FROST**

SOW DIRECT
**FROM 2-3 WEEKS
BEFORE LAST FROST**

HARDINESS
HARDY

EFFORT
○○○○○

LEGUMES

BEANS AND PEAS

Of all the vegetable groups, legumes are my favourite. Easy to grow, versatile in cooking, and delicious to eat, legumes – particularly peas and climbing beans – also add welcome vertical structure to the garden.

SOWING UNDER COVER OR DIRECT

You can sow legumes directly into their final positions but ensure the ground doesn't dry out and beware of pests. My direct-sown crops suffered rodent damage so I now start them all off under cover and transplant later.

For smaller spaces, it's best to start peas off under cover in modules but I have found that sowing them under cover in roof guttering is ideal for large crops that will grow on in a raised bed. Using this ingenious method devised by the late Geoff Hamilton, a section of roof guttering serves both as a seed tray and a transplanting tool. The method is outlined below so you can give this technique a try.

PEAS IN GUTTERING

Sow peas in roof guttering before simply sliding seedlings straight out of the gutter and into a prepared trench.

1. Take a section of roof guttering (avoid lead), cover the base with a 5–7cm (2–2¾in) layer of compost then sow 3 seeds at 2.5cm (1in) intervals along the length of the gutter.
2. Cover with 2cm (¾in) of compost and water well. Keep under cover, ideally off the ground.
3. When seedlings are around 10cm (4in) tall they are ready to be transplanted. Water well, then use a Dutch hoe to create a trench in the soil that is the same length, width, and depth as the gutter. Then, gently lay one end of the gutter at the far end of the trench and slide out the seedlings, working backwards.
4. Once the seedlings are in the trench, firm compost back around the roots, water well, and put in pea sticks or a support structure.

Sliding pea seedlings straight from a section of roof guttering into the raised bed is really satisfying.

PEA AND BEAN SHOOTS

Try growing peas for their delicious shoots, which you can harvest throughout the season and enjoy freshly picked in salads. Choose tall-growing varieties, sow in modules (not the guttering method) then transplant, leaving a space of 5–7cm (2–2¾in) between clumps of seedlings or individual plants. Harvesting the shoots when they are 5–7cm (2–2¾in) encourages the plants to branch and more shoots to form so you can enjoy continuous harvests for weeks to come. As long as you don't pick all the shoots at once, the plants will grow on to produce pods.

Young broad bean shoots also provide a leafy harvest and can be lightly steamed, blanched, or stir-fried for a delicious treat. Sow any leftover broad bean seeds thickly in a tray on a 5cm (2in) layer of compost. Cover with another 2–3cm (¾–1¼in) of compost, keep well watered, and harvest the shoots when they are around 10cm (4in) tall. For indoor harvests all year round, sow broad beans in trays on your windowsill. The same method also works for peas.

Pick tender young pea shoots little and often to maintain continuous production.

BEANS: DWARF FRENCH

Start off Sow single seeds 5cm (2in) deep in 7cm (2¾in) diameter pots, deep-celled module trays, or cardboard tubes filled with compost. Water and keep in a light, sunny position and preferably high up out of the reach of rodents.

Grow on To protect seedlings from frost, bring them indoors overnight if your polytunnel or greenhouse is too cold, or cover them with layers of horticultural fleece. Once their first true leaves are fully open and new leaves are forming, plant out seedlings 15–20cm (6–8in) apart in diagonal rows. Once flowers form, water well.

Harvest Beans are ready to pick as soon as the pods have firmed up. Don't leave them on the plant for too long: they will begin drying out and become inedible. Continue harvesting little and often, picking the ripest pods first.

SOWING DEPTH
4–5CM (1½–2IN)

SOW UNDER COVER
**FROM 2 WEEKS
BEFORE LAST FROST**

SOW DIRECT
**FROM 2–3 WEEKS
AFTER LAST FROST**

HARDINESS
HARDY

EFFORT
● ○ ○ ○ ○

SOWING DEPTH
5CM (2IN)

SOW UNDER COVER
**FROM 8-10 WEEKS
BEFORE LAST FROST**

SOW DIRECT
**FROM 3-4 WEEKS
BEFORE LAST FROST**

HARDINESS
VERY HARDY

EFFORT
●○○○○

BEANS: BROAD

Start off As for dwarf French beans.

Grow on Broad beans don't require frost protection. Once seedlings are 7–10cm (2¾–4in) tall, plant out in diagonal rows leaving 25–30cm (10–12in) between plants. As they grow, protect plants from strong winds or add extra support by tying the stems loosely to stakes. Once broad beans begin flowering in earnest, pinch out the top growing shoot (it's edible) to prevent blackfly; water well.

Harvest Broad beans are ready to harvest when the pods are plump and feel firm when gently squeezed. For sweeter-tasting beans, pick and eat them when still young before the pods have filled. Try both to see which you prefer. Continue harvesting until the plant stops flowering and producing new pods.

SOWING DEPTH
5CM (2IN)

SOW UNDER COVER
**FROM 2 WEEKS
BEFORE LAST FROST**

SOW DIRECT
**FROM 2-3 WEEKS
AFTER LAST FROST**

HARDINESS
TENDER

EFFORT
●●○○○

BEANS: RUNNER

Start off As for dwarf French beans.

Grow on Protect seedlings from frost. Build a support structure at least 1.8m (6ft) tall, such as an A-frame, trellis, or wigwam for the seedlings to grow up and ensure there is 25–30cm (10–12in) between each upright. When seedlings are at least 10cm (4in) tall, plant out 1 seedling per pole and if they fail to latch on, gently wrap the growing tip around the pole and tie loosely with string. Keep well watered, especially when plants are flowering, to promote good pod set. If the plants grow too tall, simply pinch out the growing tip.

Harvest Pick when the beans are a good length and snap easily, then steam or stir-fry. Alternatively, allow the beans to mature in the pod, remove, and cook until tender. Or, dry out the beans fully and use in stews and casseroles over autumn and winter.

SOWING DEPTH
5CM (2IN)

SOW UNDER COVER
**FROM 2 WEEKS
BEFORE LAST FROST**

SOW DIRECT
**FROM 2-3 WEEKS
AFTER LAST FROST**

HARDINESS
TENDER

EFFORT
●●○○○

BEANS: FRENCH CLIMBING

Start off As for dwarf French beans.
Grow on As for runner beans.
Harvest As for runner beans.

PEAS: GARDEN

Start off Either sow in guttering (see p106) or insert 3-4 seeds per module or 4-5 seeds per 7cm (2¾in) pot. Do not thin pea seedlings.

Grow on Follow the steps for guttering. If growing in modules or pots, first create a pea structure to match the height of the variety. A-frames and wigwams are ideal for tall varieties, while trellis or twiggy branches (peasticks) will support dwarf peas or those of intermediate height. Transplant clumps in a single row, leaving 7cm (2¾in) space between each, or in rows 15–25cm (6–10in) apart and leave 7–10cm (2¾–4in) between each clump of seedlings.

Harvest The timing of the first harvest will depend on the pea variety sown. Some early peas will be ready in 11–12 weeks, while maincrop varieties take about 16 weeks to mature.

Garden peas are ready to harvest when pods are firm to the touch. Pick just before you are ready to cook them for the freshest taste.

SOWING DEPTH
2-3CM (¾-1¼IN)

SOW UNDER COVER
**FROM 4-6 WEEKS
BEFORE LAST FROST**

SOW DIRECT
FROM AROUND LAST FROST

HARDINESS
HALF-HARDY

EFFORT
●●○○○○

PEAS: MANGETOUT

Start off As for garden peas.
Grow on As for garden peas.
Harvest Mangetout are ready when the pods have developed but the peas haven't started swelling. The pods should snap cleanly in half with no stringiness apparent.

SOWING DEPTH
2-3CM (¾-1¼IN)

SOW UNDER COVER
**FROM 4-6 WEEKS
BEFORE LAST FROST**

SOW DIRECT
FROM AROUND LAST FROST

HARDINESS
HALF-HARDY

EFFORT
●●○○○○

PEAS: SUGAR SNAP

Start off As for garden peas.
Grow on As for garden peas.
Harvest Sugar snaps are ready to harvest the moment the pod and peas feel firm. Harvest regularly to avoid both pods and peas becoming tough.

SOWING DEPTH
2-3CM (¾-1¼IN)

SOW UNDER COVER
**FROM 4-6 WEEKS
BEFORE LAST FROST**

SOW DIRECT
FROM AROUND LAST FROST

HARDINESS
HALF-HARDY

EFFORT
●●○○○○

ROOTS AND STEMS

FOR GREAT VARIETY AND TASTE

Yields from root vegetables are high in proportion to the amount of space they occupy in the garden and some also have edible leaves. Even better – given the cool, wet climate in Wales – the range of roots I can grow and enjoy is huge.

SOWING METHODS

Traditionally, roots were always sown directly into the ground, but in recent years there has been a shift towards starting them off in modules and then transplanting. Succession sowing in modules extends the season and guarantees full beds. With the exception of parsnips, potatoes, and carrots, you can choose to sow the other root crops in this section either in modules or direct. Both methods work well, and I encourage you to experiment with a variety of roots to see which works best for you.

VARIETIES

There are so many different root and stem crops to grow, from carrots to Florence fennel, so why not make the most of the fantastic choice on offer and try something new every growing season? Not only might you discover a variety that crops really well in your particular region but you'll also experience the joy of pulling yellow carrots, golden beetroot, and purple potatoes from the ground.

VERSATILITY

Root crops are very productive yet take up comparatively little space and I find them useful for filling any small gaps that emerge in my beds. When I start off root crops in modules I grow a few too many on purpose, especially beetroot, and always manage to slot them in. There is a fantastic variety of root crops available year-round, and with their different flavours and textures they are very versatile in the kitchen.

MOISTURE

Root vegetables, particularly carrots and parsnips, can be sensitive to lack of moisture. In dry conditions they become stressed and either run to seed, become woody, or provide a lacklustre crop. Conserve moisture by growing root vegetables in soils mulched with plenty of organic matter, and plant them in partial shade when possible.

Harvesting multi-sown beetroot that were planted between Swiss chard and kohlrabi.

BEETROOT

Start off Sow beetroot in rows 20–25cm (8–10in) apart, with 1 seed every 2cm (1in). Alternatively sow 4–5 seeds 2cm (1in) deep in medium-sized modules (40–50mm/1½–2in diameter).

Grow on Keep well-watered and thin direct-sown beetroot to 1 plant every 5–7cm (2–2¾in). For module-sown beetroot thin to 5 seedlings per module, and transplant once they are around 5cm tall with a spacing of 15–20cm (6–8in) between clumps.

Harvest Pull up the largest beetroot first (for both direct and module sown) to allow the smaller roots to continue growing. Pick a few young leaves for salads or stir-fries.

SOWING DEPTH
2CM (¾IN)

SOW UNDER COVER
FROM 6-8 WEEKS BEFORE LAST FROST

SOW DIRECT
FROM AROUND LAST FROST

HARDINESS
HALF HARDY (HARDY ONCE MATURED)

EFFORT
●○○○○

CARROTS

Start off Don't sow in modules for transplanting because carrot taproots are extremely fragile. Direct sow in rows at a spacing of 15cm (6in) for small, early carrots and 20cm (8in) for maincrop varieties. Sow carrot seeds as thinly as you can, ideally at around 1 seed per cm. Water well and use the plank method (see p88) to ensure successful germination.

Grow on Once seedlings appear, cover your crop with a very fine mesh to deter carrot fly (see p135 for details). Thin carrots to 1 plant every 4–5cm (1½–2in) for smaller, earlier varieties, or 5–7cm (2–2¾in) for larger.

Harvest Carrots can be pulled at any time. With early crops, harvest the largest first so the smaller carrots fill the space.

SOWING DEPTH
1-2CM (½-¾IN)

SOW UNDER COVER
FROM 4-6 WEEKS BEFORE LAST FROST (IF GROWING IN A POLYTUNNEL)

SOW DIRECT
FROM 2-3 WEEKS BEFORE LAST FROST

HARDINESS
HALF HARDY (HARDY ONCE MATURED)

EFFORT
●●○○○

KOHLRABI

Start off As for Florence fennel (see p115) but kohlrabi can be grown on in full sun.

Grow on As for Florence fennel but space seedlings 15cm (6in) apart.

Harvest I like to wait until kohlrabi is just a little bigger than a tennis ball before harvesting. Cut the head from the top of the stalk, then remove the stalk but keep the roots in the ground to benefit soil microbes. It's a good idea to sow more kohlrabi every couple of weeks to ensure continuous production.

SOWING DEPTH
1-2CM (½-¾IN)

SOW UNDER COVER
FROM 4-6 WEEKS BEFORE LAST FROST

SOW DIRECT
FROM AROUND LAST FROST

HARDINESS
HALF HARDY

EFFORT
●●●○○

PARSNIPS

Start off Parsnip seeds take a while to germinate and patience is required. Sow direct using the same spacings as for carrots but add a few extra seeds to each trench for good measure. Ensure you use the plank method (see p88) to aid germination.

Grow on Once the first seedlings are emerging under the plank, remove it and water deeply. Thin seedlings to 1 every 10cm (4in) to allow plenty of space for plants to grow and develop.

Harvest Start harvesting parsnips after the first hard frosts. You may need to use a fork to gently loosen the soil around the roots if you can't pull them out cleanly.

SOWING DEPTH
1-2CM (½-¾IN)

SOW UNDER COVER
N/A

SOW DIRECT
FROM 2-3 WEEKS BEFORE LAST FROST

HARDINESS
VERY HARDY

EFFORT

●●○○○

Whether you're growing potatoes in containers (*above*) or in raised beds (*right*) you should get a plentiful supply and they'll taste delicious!

POTATOES IN CONTAINERS

Start off You will need one 25-30 litres (5½–7¾ gallons) bucket per 2 seed potatoes. Fill to just below halfway with homemade or peat-free organic multipurpose compost. Push the first seed potato 5cm (2in) down slightly to the left of the centre of the pot, add another 10–15cm (4–6in) of compost and insert the second as before but slightly to the right of the centre. Fill the bucket with more compost and water thoroughly.

Grow on Keep plants watered and check the forecast for frost. If cold temperatures threaten, either bring the containers under cover or rig up a simple covering (see p145).

Harvest Lift first early potatoes a couple of weeks after they start flowering and about 10–12 weeks after sowing, and second earlies 12–14 weeks after sowing. Let maincrop potatoes start to die back first before harvesting. Gently tip out the entire contents of the bucket into an empty wheelbarrow and pick out the potatoes.

POTATOES IN RAISED BEDS

Start off Create a 20cm (8in) deep planting hole using a trowel, and drop in some of your best compost to fill the first 5cm (2in) of the hole. Place a seed potato on top, add 1–2 litres (1¾–2½ pints) of water then cover with the soil you dug out. Plant first and second early potatoes 25–30cm (10–12in) apart, and maincrop varieties 30cm (12in) apart. Rows should be 30cm (12in) apart and seed potatoes staggered to maximize space below ground.

Grow on First and second earlies don't need to be earthed up, but you can do this for maincrop potatoes. Rather than raking soil from the bed up and over the plants, cover emerging foliage with a 10cm (4in) mound of compost, well-decomposed woodchip or leaf mould. Protect from frost with two layers of fleece.

Harvest Follow timings given for container-grown potatoes. Gently pull out the plants and use your hands to find any potatoes still in the ground. Rake the bed flat once the

crop has been harvested and water with homemade LAB (see p140) to help restore soil health after the disturbance.

SOWING DEPTH
15–20CM (6–8IN)

SOW UNDER COVER
CHIT SEED POTATOES FROM 2–3 WEEKS BEFORE PLANTING

SOW DIRECT
FROM 5–6 WEEKS BEFORE LAST FROST

HARDINESS
TENDER

EFFORT
●●●○○

RADISH

Start off Sow direct in trenches at 1–2 seeds per cm and space rows 10cm (4in) apart. For module sowings, sow 5–7 seeds per cell.

Grow on Thinning to 1 seedling every 2–3cm (¾–1 ¼in) is necessary only for direct-sown seeds. Plant out clumps of module-sown seedlings 7–10cm (2¾–4in) apart, and leave 10cm (4in) between rows.

Harvest Pick radish around 4–5 weeks after sowing for fresh, crunchy roots. If you've sown more than you can eat, leave plants to produce pretty white, edible flowers and then set seed. Enjoy eating the seed pods while they are still green.

SOWING DEPTH
1–2CM (½–¾IN)

SOW UNDER COVER
FROM 4 WEEKS BEFORE LAST FROST

SOW DIRECT
FROM 1–2 WEEKS BEFORE LAST FROST

HARDINESS
HARDY

EFFORT
●○○○○

SOWING DEPTH
2CM (¾IN)

SOW UNDER COVER
**FROM 5–6 WEEKS
BEFORE LAST FROST**

SOW DIRECT
**FROM 1–2 WEEKS
BEFORE LAST FROST**

HARDINESS
VERY HARDY

EFFORT
●●○○○

SWEDE

Start off Sow in trenches at a spacing of 1 seed every 2cm (¾in) and leave 15–20cm (6–8in) between rows. Sow 1–2 seeds per module and thin to the strongest seedling.

Grow on For large swedes, thin seedlings to 1 every 10cm (4in), or reduce the space to 7cm (2¾in) for smaller roots. When transplanting from modules, use the same spacings and leave 15–20cm (6–8in) between rows.

Harvest Start lifting swedes after the first autumn frosts and continue harvesting through the winter. Swedes store exceptionally well in the ground so harvest as needed.

SOWING DEPTH
1–2CM (½–¾IN)

SOW UNDER COVER
**FROM 4 WEEKS
BEFORE LAST FROST**

SOW DIRECT
**FROM 1–2 WEEKS
BEFORE LAST FROST**

HARDINESS
HARDY

EFFORT
●○○○○

TURNIPS

Start off Direct sowing as for radish. In modules sow 3-4 seeds per cell.

Grow on As for winter radish.

Harvest You can start lifting young turnips, which have a fresh, mild taste, as soon as 6–8 weeks after sowing, or leave them to develop in size. For a supply of roots through the winter, start off seedlings in early summer (as for winter radish). Any left in the ground will sprout early the following spring - the new leaves are delicious.

SOWING DEPTH
1–2CM (½–¾IN)

SOW UNDER COVER
FROM EARLY SUMMER

SOW DIRECT
FROM EARLY SUMMER

HARDINESS
HARDY

EFFORT
●○○○○

WINTER RADISH

Start off As for radish.

Grow on Thin to 1 seedling every 5cm (2in) or transplant module-sown clumps 10–12cm (4–4¾in) apart.

Harvest Pull the first radishes around 8 weeks from sowing and leave the others in the ground for harvests from autumn to late winter.

CELERY

Start off Sow celery seeds very thinly in a seed tray, covering with just a touch of compost. Place on a heated mat or in a plant propagator to aid germination, which takes a while. Once seedlings have emerged, gently pot on into medium-sized modules or 7cm (2¾in) pots and let them grow on to produce a few true leaves. If the temperature falls below 9–10°C (48–50°F) and is set to stay low for 6–8 hours, move them to a warmer spot until temperatures rise again. This is because low temperatures can lead to bolting.

Grow on Before transplanting, harden off the seedlings for 4–5 days in a cloche or coldframe, then transplant once there is no risk of frost. Add a generous handful of homemade compost to the base of each planting hole and space plants and rows 25–30cm (10–12in) apart. Water deeply and continue to keep celery well-watered as they grow.

Harvest There are two ways you can harvest celery: the first is to pull off individual stems and allow the smaller ones to continue developing; the second is to cut off the whole head just below the base.

SOWING DEPTH
0.5CM (¼IN)

SOW UNDER COVER
**FROM 8-10 WEEKS
BEFORE LAST FROST**

SOW DIRECT
N/A

HARDINESS
TENDER

EFFORT
●●●●○

CELERIAC

Start off As for celery.
Grow on As for celery but transplant leaving 30–35cm (12–14in) between plants and rows.
Harvest Harvest celeriac from October onwards by gently lifting the roots. Choose the larger roots first and leave the rest of the crop in the ground. Harvest as and when needed throughout the rest of autumn and into winter.

SOWING DEPTH
0.5CM (¼IN)

SOW UNDER COVER
**FROM 8-10 WEEKS
BEFORE LAST FROST**

SOW DIRECT
N/A

HARDINESS
HALF HARDY

EFFORT
●●●○○

FLORENCE FENNEL

Start off Sow fennel in modules or direct. For modules sow 1–2 seeds per cell and thin to the strongest seedling. Direct sow thinly (1 seed every 2cm/¾in) in trenches, leaving a space of 20cm (8in) between rows. Fennel is a cool-weather crop, and for good bulb production it's best grown in areas that are partially shaded from hot summer sun.
Grow on Transplant 1 seedling every 10cm (4in), or every 15cm (6in) if you want larger bulbs.

Space rows of seedlings roughly 20cm (8in) apart and stagger the plants so they create a diagonal pattern in the bed. Thin direct-sown seedlings to the same distance: 1 every 20cm (8in).
Harvest Harvest fennel by cutting off the bulb at ground level when it reaches the desired size, usually around 3–4 months after sowing.

SOWING DEPTH
1-2CM (½-¾IN)

SOW UNDER COVER
**FROM 3-4 WEEKS
BEFORE LAST FROST**

SOW DIRECT
**FROM 1-2 WEEKS
BEFORE LAST FROST**

HARDINESS
HALF HARDY

EFFORT
●●○○○

ALLIUMS

THE ONION FAMILY

Indispensable in the kitchen, alliums are my favourite vegetable for adding depth of flavour to savoury dishes. In recent years I've been growing them in larger quantities and testing out the varieties most suited to the climate here.

ALLIUMS ARE SO VERSATILE WHEN IT COMES TO COOKING AS THEY ADD SO MUCH FLAVOUR TO A HUGE RANGE OF DISHES.

QUANITFY YOUR HARVEST

It's easy to calculate how much you can expect to harvest from a given area when planting alliums. With garlic and leeks, for example, one plant equals one harvest and the specific spacing allows you to calculate how much you need to grow to last a whole year. Based on your average consumption, you can plan how many plants to sow to keep your family supplied through the winter. See page 168 for further advice on growing for self-sufficiency.

VERSATILITY IN THE KITCHEN

I like to get creative in the kitchen with alliums and find as many ways to use and eat them as possible. Below are three examples of simple ways to get more from one crop.

Onion leaves

These make a great alternative to spring onions when a salad or a topping needs a little extra kick. Choose one healthy leaf per plant and chop up finely.

Spring and salad onions

Once I've harvested a few, I like to let both types of onion grow on to develop bigger bulbs. They may be smaller than regular onions, but they have a nice, fairly mild flavour.

Leeks

Although they may not cook down in the same way as onions, leeks make fantastic substitutes and the flavour is excellent. When cooking, try replacing one medium onion with one medium leek.

ONION SETS OR SEEDS?

Growing onions from seed under cover allows you to multisow and it also tends to give better yields. However, I am a huge fan of growing from sets, which is less time-consuming than starting off onion seeds on a heat mat. I much prefer and enjoy the more straightforward process of planting and transplanting the sets.

DON'T FORGET THE FLOWERS

The allium family yields some of the most amazing flowers and these will attract beneficial insects to your plot to pollinate crops. Rather than harvesting every single leek or garlic bulb, why not let one or two develop a beautiful flower head? You won't be disappointed.

Leave some leeks to flower so you and the pollinating insects can enjoy their beautiful, dramatic heads.

SOWING DEPTH
5-6CM (2-2½IN)

SOW UNDER COVER
N/A

SOW DIRECT
FROM EARLY AUTUMN

HARDINESS
VERY HARDY

EFFORT
●●●●●

GARLIC

Start off Sow garlic cloves in diagonal rows 5cm (2in) deep and allow 7–8cm (2¾–3in) between cloves. I tend to start in early autumn, but you can sow as late as early winter.
Grow on Mulch the garlic bed with a 2–3cm (¾–1¼in) layer of compost in late winter (as part of the general soil-building strategy for your garden).

Harvest Pull up garlic when the bottom 3–4 leaves have turned brown – usually in mid-summer. Firmly grip the base of the stem but uproot gently.

SOWING DEPTH
1-2CM (½-¾IN)

SOW UNDER COVER
FROM 8-10 WEEKS BEFORE LAST FROST

SOW DIRECT
FROM 2-3 WEEKS BEFORE LAST FROST

HARDINESS
HARDY TO VERY HARDY (VARIETY DEPENDANT)

EFFORT
●●●●●

LEEKS

Start off You can start leeks under cover, sowing 3-4 seeds per module and transplanting when 5–7cm (2–2¾in) tall but I prefer to sow in a seedbed. For direct sowing, create a trench around 1–2cm (½–¾in) deep and sow thickly (2–3 seeds every 1cm/½in) – no need to thin. Use the plank method (see p88) to aid germination and be patient: seedlings take a few weeks to appear.
Grow on Remove the plank once seedlings appear and let them grow to around pencil thickness, which will take around 10 weeks. Gently lift the seedlings using a fork, and immediately place in a bucket of water to hydrate them and separate the roots. Use a narrow pointed tool, such as a dibber, to make holes 20–25cm (8–10in) deep, spacing each

hole and each row 10cm (4in) apart. Drop the seedling into the hole and water well. There is no need to push the compost back over the hole.
Harvest Uproot leeks from mid- to late autumn, depending on when they

were transplanted. If you choose a late or hardy variety, you can harvest leeks right up to early spring the following year. Grip firmly and uproot, or if the ground is a little firm use a fork to gently loosen the soil.

SOWING DEPTH
1CM (½IN)

SOW UNDER COVER
FROM 10-12 WEEKS BEFORE LAST FROST

SOW DIRECT
FROM 2-3 WEEKS BEFORE LAST FROST

HARDINESS
HARDY

EFFORT
●●●●●

ONIONS (FROM SEED)

Start off Sow 4-5 onion seeds per module and cover with a light sprinkling of compost. If you are starting as early as late winter, I recommend placing the module trays on a heat mat or in a heated propagator to kick-start the germination process. Once seedlings appear, transfer them to a greenhouse or polytunnel.

Grow on Do not thin. Once seedlings are at least 7cm (2¾in) tall, you can transplant them into their final growing position. Space clumps of seedlings 15–20cm (6–8in) apart, using the same spacing between rows.
Harvest Onions are ready to harvest when they have formed a good-sized bulb and some leaves are beginning to turn yellow – usually in mid-summer.

ONIONS (FROM SETS)

Start off Plant 1 onion set per module (cells should be around 40–50mm/1½–2in wide), making sure that the pointed end is facing upwards. If you are growing on a smaller scale, insert 1 set per 5–7cm (2–2¾in) pot.
Grow on Transplant onion sets when they are around 10cm (4in) tall, at a spacing of around 15cm (6in) between each plant and row.
Harvest As for onions from seed.

SOWING DEPTH
HALF TO TWO-THIRDS DEPTH OF SET

SOW UNDER COVER
FROM 8–10 WEEKS BEFORE LAST FROST

SOW DIRECT
FROM 3–4 WEEKS BEFORE LAST FROST

HARDINESS
HARDY

EFFORT
● ○ ○ ○ ○

ONIONS (SALAD)

Start off As for onions from seed but sow 6–7 seeds per module. Providing heat to encourage germination is highly recommended.
Grow on As for onions from seed but transplant a little closer, leaving 10cm (4in) between clumps and rows.
Harvest Start picking as soon as 8–10 weeks from sowing, once salad onions are around pencil thickness or 15cm (6in) tall. Always take the largest salad onion first to allow the smaller ones in the clump to continue growing.

SOWING DEPTH
1CM (½IN)

SOW UNDER COVER
FROM 8–10 WEEKS BEFORE LAST FROST

SOW DIRECT
FROM 3–4 WEEKS BEFORE LAST FROST

HARDINESS
HARDY

EFFORT
● ● ○ ○ ○

SHALLOTS

Start off Plant out shallot sets at a spacing of 20cm (8in) between bulbs, and 25cm (10in) between rows. You may need to cover these initially with netting to stop them being uprooted by birds. Remove the netting when plants are growing strongly. Alternatively plant under cover, inserting 1 set per cell in a larger module tray or 7cm (2¾in) pot.

Grow on Transplant module/pot-grown shallots when the leaves are 7–10cm (2¾–4in) tall.
Harvest A single shallot set will turn into a clump of shallot bulbs. These are ready to harvest when the foliage starts turning yellow or brown.

SOWING DEPTH
HALF TO TWO-THIRDS DEPTH OF SET

SOW UNDER COVER
FROM 8–10 WEEKS BEFORE LAST FROST

SOW DIRECT
FROM 3–4 WEEKS BEFORE LAST FROST

HARDINESS
VERY HARDY

EFFORT
● ○ ○ ○ ○

SALADS

EASY-TO-GROW FRESH LEAVES

In terms of space requirement compared to size of yield, salads are perhaps the most productive crop in the vegetable plot. They don't root deeply, are quick to mature, and perfect for container growing.

PICK SALAD JUST BEFORE YOU PLAN TO EAT IT. THE FLAVOUR OF THE FRESH LEAVES IS FANTASTIC.

CUT-AND-COME-AGAIN LEAVES

To ensure a continuous supply of fresh leaves for minimum effort grow salads as cut-and-come-again crops. All the vegetables in this section are suited to this method – even lettuce that are listed as "hearting" varieties will work. The best way to grow cut-and-come again leaves is by sowing direct, keeping plants well watered and sowing a new row every 2–3 weeks to ensure a continuous supply throughout the season.

HOW MUCH TO GROW?

For a household of two adults, an area measuring 1.2m x 1.2m (4ft x 4ft) dedicated exclusively to salad crops will supply your needs from spring through to mid-autmn. For a family of four, simply double the size of the area. Try it for a growing season then make any necessary adjustments. However much salad you grow, you must protect your crops with a fleece covering at both the start and the end of the season (see pp144–147).

SHADE IN SUMMER

The season when most of us want to pick and eat homegrown salads is summer, but these crops don't respond well to hot, dry weather. It lowers the quality of the leaf and can also cause the plants to become stressed and bolt. The solution is to dedicate a partially shaded area of your plot to salads and avoid growing them in full sun during high summer. A degree of shade not only reduces water evaporation, but also keeps temperatures cooler, which will help to prolong the harvesting period for the salad you grow.

OVERWINTERING

Although salad leaves are delicate, many are surprisingly hardy and will overwinter when grown in a polytunnel. Mid-summer is the prime time to sow winter lettuce varieties. Start them off in modules and then transplant once summer crops, such as tomatoes, have been removed. Growth will slow down in midwinter but pick up again in late winter, giving you a fantastic yield at the start of the "hungry gap" in early spring (see p158).

SALAD AS GREEN MANURE

Don't waste empty space in your beds towards the end of the growing season. Simply broadcast (sprinkle over the soil) any leftover salad seeds and cover with a light layer of compost. The resulting plants will act as "green manure" – a crop sown to cover bare soil then dug back in to enrich it. Digging, however, isn't necessary: just hoe off the top growth then return it to the soil using "chop and drop" (see p66). When salad plants die down, you can remove the leaves to compost but keep the roots in the ground to help maintain soil health and fertility.

INTERCROPPING

Use intercropping to add variety and make your salad bed look much more interesting. Simply transplant modules of different salad plants 10–15cm (4–6in) apart, such as red lettuce varieties intercropped with spinach.

Started off in modules (*top left*) then transplanted (*top right*), salads are soon ready to harvest on a cut-and-come again basis (*right*).

SOWING DEPTH
1CM (½IN)

SOW UNDER COVER
FROM EARLY SUMMER

SOW DIRECT
FROM EARLY SUMMER

HARDINESS
HALF-HARDY

EFFORT
● ○ ○ ○ ○

CHICORY

Start off There are different types of chicory and ways to grow them. This is the simplest method using red chicory (radicchio), which will give you great harvests for autumn. Sow seeds thinly in rows 20–25cm (8–10in) apart. To start off chicory in modules, follow the instructions for lettuce (below).

Grow on Once chicory seedlings appear, thin to 25–30cm (10–12in) between plants for heads of chicory, or leave just 5–7cm (2–2¾in) between them for salad leaves.

Harvest When chicory leaves are the size you want, use the cut-and-come again method. Harvest chicory heads when firm by cutting off the head at ground level.

SOWING DEPTH
1CM (½IN)

SOW UNDER COVER
**FROM 8–10 WEEKS
BEFORE LAST FROST**

SOW DIRECT
**FROM 2–3 WEEKS
BEFORE LAST FROST**

HARDINESS
**HALF-HARDY TO HARDY
(VARIETY DEPENDANT)**

EFFORT
● ○ ○ ○ ○

LETTUCE

Start off As for direct-sown chicory but with less space between rows. For cut-and-come-again leaves allow 15cm (6in). For heads of lettuce, start off seeds under cover by sowing thickly in a seed tray. Carefully prick out once seedlings have 2 true leaves, and transplant 1 seedling per medium-sized module (40–50mm/1½–2in wide).

Grow on Transplant module-sown lettuce when seedlings have 7–8 true leaves, allowing 25cm (10in) between plants, and 25–30cm (10–12in) between rows. There is no need to thin direct-sown lettuce grown as a cut-and-come again crop.

Harvest Pick heads when large and firm, and harvest leaves little and often. Sow a new row of lettuce seeds every 3 weeks to maintain a constant supply.

SOWING DEPTH
1CM (½IN)

SOW UNDER COVER
**FROM 7–8 WEEKS
BEFORE LAST FROST**

SOW DIRECT
**FROM 2–3 WEEKS
BEFORE LAST FROST**

HARDINESS
(VARIETY DEPENDANT)

EFFORT
● ○ ○ ○ ○

MUSTARD GREENS

Start off Although you can start off mustard greens in modules, sowing direct is much simpler. Sow thinly in rows spaced 15–20cm (6–8in) apart.

Grow on There is no need to thin quick-growing mustard greens but keep them well watered.

Harvest Pick mustard greens on a cut-and-come again basis, selecting the larger leaves first.

ROCKET

Start off As for mustard greens. Rocket grows particularly well when sown direct in late summer.
Grow on As for mustard greens.
Harvest As for mustard greens.

SOWING DEPTH
1–2CM (½–¾IN)

SOW UNDER COVER
FROM 7–8 WEEKS BEFORE LAST FROST

SOW DIRECT
FROM AROUND LAST FROST

HARDINESS
HARDY

EFFORT
● ○ ○ ○ ○

SPINACH

Start off Either sow direct or in modules. For baby leaves sow direct in trenches with 1 seed roughly every 1cm (½in) and 15cm (6in) between rows. For larger leaves, sow 1–2 seeds per medium-sized module.
Grow on There is no need to thin direct-sown spinach. Transplant module-grown seedlings 7cm (2¾in) apart and allow 15cm (6in) between rows.
Harvest Pick spinach on a cut-and-come again basis choosing the larger leaves first.

SOWING DEPTH
2CM (¾IN)

SOW UNDER COVER
FROM 7–8 WEEKS BEFORE LAST FROST

SOW DIRECT
FROM AROUND LAST FROST

HARDINESS
HARDY

EFFORT
● ○ ○ ○ ○

SWISS CHARD

Start off As for chicory if sowing direct for baby leaves, but deeper and allow 20-25cm (8–10in) between rows. You can also start off Swiss chard in modules, sowing 1–2 seeds per module for stems, and 3–4 seeds for baby leaves.
Grow on Thinning Swiss chard sown direct for baby leaves isn't necessary. For stems and large leaves thin to 20cm (8in) between plants and use the same measurement when transplanting module-grown

seedlings. When transplanting clumps of Swiss chard for salad leaves, space them roughly 7cm (2¾in) apart.
Harvest Pick baby leaves as you need them using the cut-and-come again method. Allow leaves and stems for cooking to grow to the size you want and harvest the biggest first, allowing the smaller stems to continue growing.

SOWING DEPTH
2–3CM (¾–1¼IN)

SOW UNDER COVER
FROM 7–8 WEEKS BEFORE LAST FROST

SOW DIRECT
FROM AROUND LAST FROST

HARDINESS
HARDY

EFFORT
● ○ ○ ○ ○

FRUITING VEGETABLES

SUN-LOVING CROPS FOR SUMMER HARVESTS

This group includes very tender crops, such as tomatoes, that must be started off under cover. All need warmth and sunshine to fruit successfully but where summers are not reliably hot, sowing at the right time is crucial.

EXTRA LIGHT AND HEAT

I rely on heated propagators to get the majority of my fruiting crops started early, otherwise there is a high probability that the plants won't be fully mature by the time the cooler autumn weather arrives. Heat mats under trays or pots of seedlings create constant warmth or you could try a heated propagator. Both can be placed on a sunny windowsill or under grow lights. These additional heating and lighting sources are relatively inexpensive and can be used throughout the year to start off other crops such as microgreens.

GERMINATING SQUASH

For successful germination, my preferred method is to sow squash seeds on moist paper towels in a heated propagator. Mist seeds daily and when they germinate, gently tear the paper around the sprouted seeds and plant each sprouted seed at a depth of 1–2cm (½–¾in) in individual pots or modules.

HARDENING OFF

Tender fruiting vegetable seedlings must be hardened off before you plant them out to lessen the shock of cooler temperatures at night. Take your seedlings outside in the

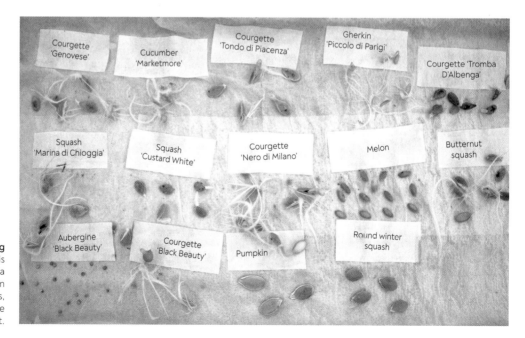

Germinating fruiting vegetable seeds is much easier with a propagator. Sown on damp paper towels, most of my seeds are starting to shoot.

Courgettes are fast growers. If you've got far more than you can eat, share harvests with friends and neighbours.

morning to a bright but sheltered area, and gradually bring them in a little later each night. Follow this procedure for around 5–7 days and the plants will be acclimatized.

WATERING AND FLAVOUR

How much and how regularly you water tomatoes and peppers can influence taste and spiciness respectively. Watering plants less often intensifies the flavour of tomatoes and the heat of peppers. Try this for yourself by withholding water from 2 or 3 plants 3 weeks after picking the first few tomatoes from them. You'll get fewer tomatoes but the amazing taste will be worth it. For spicier peppers, reduce watering around 2–3 weeks before the majority will be ready to harvest.

GLUTS

Given the short season of fruiting vegetables, you are likely to experience gluts. Having an abundance of tomatoes isn't an issue because you can cook and freeze them, but a glut of courgettes is a different matter. The solution is simple: plant fewer courgettes next season and give the space to other crops. Gluts can, of course, inspire us to be creative in the kitchen, but they can also feel overwhelming. Prioritize one crop at a time to process and preserve, which will most likely be tomatoes, and consult the Gift of Giving (see p210) for creative ways with gluts.

AUBERGINE

Start off Sow 2 seeds per 7cm (2¾in) pot or module and cover with a shallow layer of compost. Place on a heated mat or in a propagator and add grow lights for stronger plants.
Grow on Thin to the strongest seedling and continue growing under cover, moving the seedling into a bigger pot if the weather is still too cold for planting out. Once there has been no frost for at least 3–4 weeks, move seedlings into a polytunnel or greenhouse; alternatively cover with a cloche. Harden seedlings off then make planting holes twice the depth of the pot, fill the bottom half with high-quality compost and water well. Transplant the young aubergines, teasing out any congested roots and space 50-60cm (20–24in) apart. Pinch out the growing tip when 30cm (12in) tall to encourage a bushy shape. Stake at this point to provide support for the heavy fruits. If you are growing the larger cultivars, remove new flowers once 6 fruits have set.
Harvest Pick aubergines when they are firm and with a beautiful shine on their skin.

SOWING DEPTH
ON THE SURFACE

SOW UNDER COVER
FROM 8–10 WEEKS BEFORE LAST FROST

HARDINESS
TENDER

EFFORT
●●●●○

SOWING DEPTH
1–2CM (½–¾IN)

SOW UNDER COVER
**FROM 4 WEEKS
BEFORE LAST FROST**

HARDINESS
TENDER

EFFORT
●●○○○

COURGETTES AND SUMMER SQUASH

Start off Sow seeds on moist paper towel (see p124). Once germinated, grow on courgette seedlings in an under cover space such as a mini-greenhouse but bring plants indoors if there is a risk of frost. Plants grow very quickly so can be started off later than other fruiting crops.
Grow on Once seedlings have at least 3–4 true leaves and the risk of frost has passed, plant them out into their final growing positions. Non-trailing courgettes and squash should be spaced around 90cm (3ft) apart to accommodate their large leaves. Trailing varieties need a spread of at least 2–3m (6½–10ft) for their long sideshoots or you can train these up a trellis. Provide support for heavier fruit by tying a soft strap around the fruit and attaching it to the trellis, leaving space for further fruit to grow. Keep squash well watered; they're thirsty plants!
Harvest Courgettes are ready to harvest when they are the size you want. Always pick the largest fruits to allow the smaller ones to grow on. Cut off squash leaving at least 5cm (2in) of stalk still attached to help prolong storage. Harvest all fruits before the first frost.

SOWING DEPTH
1–2CM (½–¾IN)

SOW UNDER COVER
**FROM 4–6 WEEKS
BEFORE LAST FROST**

HARDINESS
TENDER

EFFORT
●●●○○

CUCUMBER

Start off As for courgettes and summer squash.
Grow on As for courgettes and summer squash but cucumbers perform best if trained vertically. Either allow them to grow up a trellis or up thick strings attached to the top of a polytunnel. You could also create a "pyramid frame" and place 1 plant in each of the 4 corners. When growing vertically, aim to space plants 30–40cm (12–16in) apart.

Harvest For the best-tasting fruit, pick cucumbers before they get too large.

SOWING DEPTH
ON THE SURFACE

SOW UNDER COVER
**FROM 10–12 WEEKS
BEFORE LAST FROST**

HARDINESS
TENDER

EFFORT
●●●●○

PEPPERS
(SWEET AND CHILLI)

Start off As for aubergines.
Grow on As for aubergines but space sweet pepper plants 40–45cm (16–18in) apart and chilli peppers 30–35cm (12–14in) apart, pinching out the growing tips of both types when they are 20cm (8in) tall.
Harvest As soon as the first fruits mature, pick them regularly so the plants continue fruiting into autumn.

PUMPKIN AND WINTER SQUASH

Start off As for courgettes and summer squash.

Grow on As for courgettes and summer squash.

Harvest Cut winter squash when they have reached a good size with the desired skin colour. If any fruit haven't matured before the first frost, harvest and continue ripening on a sunny windowsill, in a polytunnel, or a greenhouse. As with summer squash, make sure each fruit has at least 5cm (2in) of stem still attached.

SOWING DEPTH
1–2CM (½–¾IN)

SOW UNDER COVER
FROM AROUND LAST FROST

HARDINESS
TENDER

EFFORT
●●○○○

SWEETCORN

Start off Sow sweetcorn in medium-sized modules or pots at a depth of 2–3cm (¾–1¼in). For best results place these in a heated propagator until plants are at least 5cm (2in) tall. You will need at least 12 plants for successful pollination, so aim to double this quantity when sowing.

Grow on After the risk of frost has passed, harden off and transplant seedlings in a block rather than a row. If you're growing 12 plants aim for a block of 3 x 4 (or 4 x 5 for 20 plants). Allow 45cm (18in) between each plant and give them a sunny but sheltered spot. Sweetcorn is a very thirsty crop, so keep on top of watering during dry weather.

Harvest When the furry tassels at the end of the corn turn brown, the cobs are ready to harvest. If possible, aim to pick the cobs just before you cook them for unbeatable flavour and freshness.

SOWING DEPTH
2–3CM (¾–1¼IN)

SOW UNDER COVER
**FROM 4 WEEKS
BEFORE LAST FROST**

HARDINESS
TENDER

EFFORT
●●●○○

TOMATOES

Start off Sow a few seeds per module indoors. I recommend a heated propagator with grow lights to avoid seedlings becoming leggy. When the first 2 true leaves appear lift each seedling out gently with a pencil and transfer to a 7cm (2¾in) pot or module and grow on in a light spot under cover. If late frosts are forecast, bring seedlings indoors from polytunnels. You can keep plants on a sunny windowsill or under grow lights until ready to be transplanted. If you don't have grow lights and seedlings are leggy, bury the whole stem to just above the small pair of leaves when potting on.

Grow on Create a hole twice as wide and deep as the pot, half fill with your best homemade compost, and water thoroughly. Transplant the seedling to just below the first leaf, add more compost, firm in with your hand, then water again. Provide a tall stake for support or loosely tie a piece of soft, thick string at the base of the stem and wrap it in a spiral around the plant. You then tie this to an overhead support in a polytunnel or greenhouse. Harden off outdoor varieties then plant out once all risk of frost has passed and provide support. Remember to pinch out the sideshoots (suckers) of cordon (indeterminate) varieties of tomato. This will concentrate the plant's energy on fruit production.

Harvest Tomatoes are ready when they are a good colour and the flesh gives slightly when squeezed.

SOWING DEPTH
0.5–1CM (¼–½IN)

SOW UNDER COVER
**FROM 6–8 WEEKS
BEFORE LAST FROST**

HARDINESS
TENDER

EFFORT
●●●○○

ELIMINATING
ISSUES

Nip any problems in the bud with preventative measures and top tips

THE LEARNING CURVE

PROBLEM-SOLVING IN THE GARDEN

In gardening, not everything goes acording to plan – however experienced you are. I view failure as an inevitable part of the learning process and treat it as a golden opportunity to improve my understanding.

THE BEST TIME TO LEARN FROM A GARDENING FAILURE IS THE SECOND YOU'VE NOTICED IT.

A great quote sums up my attitude to setbacks in the garden: "Failure is not the opposite of success: it's part of success" (Arianna Huffington). Whenever I encounter a crop failure, I run through all the potential causes and then eliminate any that definitely don't apply until I'm left with one, possibly two primary reasons. Causes might be weather conditions, sowing time, soil quality, pests, or lack of moisture. Once I've discovered the root cause, I know what to look out for in future growing seasons to prevent a repeat. Sometimes, however, the unexpected happens and a crop is damaged by a freak hail storm or an unexpected frost. At such times I remind myself that nature is nature after all – this helps keep me grounded and able to overcome obstacles.

HELP IS AT HAND

Failures can often teach us a lot more than successes because they force us to take a very close look at the issue. When I don't fully understand why something didn't work out, I see this as an opportunity to fill a gap in my knowledge through more reading and research. And if I still can't find the answer, I ask other people. Online gardening groups are an excellent resource for problem solving because someone, somewhere is bound to have experienced the same issue and there will often be a helpful photo. Gardeners from all over the world post on these groups and sometimes the advice may be conflicting or not relevant to your climate, but keep an open mind. Once you've tried one or two methods, you'll usually find a remedy that works in your garden. I am constantly stunned by the generosity of gardeners in online groups who freely share their knowledge and advice.

PLANT HEALTH CHECK

A simple step you can take to identify issues and lessen the chance of future crop failure is to conduct regular plant health checks. Once or twice a week, I wander around the garden and look very closely at each group of plants, carefully turning over leaves to look at the underside, examining the stems or flowers, and checking more than one specimen. Using this method, I recently averted a disaster with my swedes – a long-term crop to which I don't usually pay too much attention. On this occasion, I examined the leaves and noticed an infestation of cabbage white caterpillars. Fortunately, I had time to remove the caterpillars before they stripped the leaves bare, which would have resulted in a poorer, stunted crop. It's a good idea to take your gardener's notebook with you (see p40) when carrying out plant health checks. By noting down what you find, what the weather conditions were like, and what action you need to take, you are building up a bespoke resource that will prove invaluable on your food-growing journey.

TIP

IF THE WORST HAPPENS AND YOU COME ACROSS IRREVERSIBLE PEST OR DISEASE DAMAGE, THEN IMMEDIATELY REMOVE THAT CROP AND PLANT SOMETHING ELSE.

These spaghetti squash leaves (*top*) show no signs of pests or disease, but weather conditions may have caused marks on the bean foliage (*right*). In such cases, first remove affected leaves then the whole plant if the problem persists after two weeks.

YEAR-ROUND WEED CONTROL

STAYING ON TOP OF WEEDS

I consider weeds to be volunteer plants growing in the wrong place. There are plenty of dandelions in my paths, for example, which I leave for pollinators early in the year, but my raised beds are strictly no-go areas for weeds.

For efficient weed management, it's best to adopt a "little but often" approach so you catch troublesome weeds before they take hold. The difference between a week-old and a month-old weed is significant, and the latter takes a lot more effort to remove! I like to do regular weed blitzes of the raised beds and containers using the three key tools below and I follow this routine throughout the year.

Oscillating hoe

Also called a stirrup hoe, this fantastic long-handled tool is ideal for weeding large sections or inbetween rows of seedlings in raised beds. It makes light work of weeds and doesn't strain your back. Run the sharp two-way blade 1–2cm (½–¾in) beneath the surface of the soil and slice through weeds. I recommend the version with a 13–14cm (5–5½in) wide head.

Hand hoe

My favourite weeding tool, a hand hoe with a single blade is perfect for controlled, targeted weeding around plants. Run the blade just below soil level, as with the oscillating hoe, to clear weeds quickly and efficiently from small areas.

My hands

Robust, precise, and free to use, hands are perfect for removing small weeds as and when you see them. I tend to hand-weed as I walk round the garden, always on the lookout for creeping buttercup – my weed nemesis. Apart from dandelions in the paths, there are also clumps of nettles in and around my garden. I explain why this is my favourite weed on page 196.

CREATE A ROUTINE

Personally, I weed roughly once a week, but try to establish a routine that works for you. I make the weeding session more enjoyable by putting on headphones and listening to a podcast episode or two (see p208). What I used to consider a chore has now become a more positive experience because I look forward to immersing myself in interesting programmes. As the season progresses, you will spend less time weeding because the strong growth of crops will outcompete emerging weeds.

As part of my annual weeding strategy I also cover empty raised beds over winter (see p68). Excluding light suppresses weed growth so you can plant straight into your beds the following spring without having to weed them first.

WHEN TO WEED

Try and avoid weeding on rainy days, or just before rainfall. The faster weeds wilt, the quicker they die so choose a windy or sunny day and weed before midday when the sun is at its hottest. When hoeing has pulled up weeds with their stem and roots still intact, they will occasionally regrow. Left to dry out, however, they are more likely to wilt before they can take root again.

TIP

FROM MID-AUGUST ONWARDS KEEP A LOOKOUT FOR WEEDS APPEARING IN BEDS, ESPECIALLY WHEN COOL, DAMP WEATHER ARRIVES.

When transplanting crops, leave enough space between rows so you can hoe between them (*top left*); use a small hand hoe for gentle weeding around seedlings (*above*); and get into the habit of pulling weeds whenever you spot them (*left*).

PESTS

BUILD NATURAL DEFENCES

Using chemicals to control garden pests compromises soil health, leading to further pest and disease issues down the line. Growing a diverse range of plants and taking the preventative measures outlined below is a more effective strategy.

Pests are inevitable in any garden but I am strongly against the use of chemical controls. My preference is to cultivate diversity and to build up soil health. Pests tend to attack weak plants, which are easy targets, so additional measures, such as applying homemade mineral feeds (see pp140–141 and pp178–181), will improve resilience. For each of the common garden pests listed, there is a safe, effective alternative to chemical controls.

A. Aphids (Greenfly and blackfly)

Aphids often target the newest growth. Broad bean tips are blackfly magnets, so prevent infestations by pinching out the growing tips once plants begin flowering. A few aphids aren't a cause for concern, but if a plant is covered, blast them off with a strong jet of water, or remove the affected plant and rub off any aphids you see on neighbouring plants. Aphid numbers often surge in early spring but when natural predators, such as ladybird larvae, become more active the numbers fall. A patch of nettles will lure the aphids away from broad beans and also attract ladybirds (see p196).

B. Flea beetle

In spring, especially when conditions are dry, flea beetles can be rife on brassica crops, making holes in the leaves that can stunt growth. I've found flea-beetle damage also weakens hardy plants that are exposed to late-spring frosts. Prevent attacks by covering direct-sown brassica seedlings with a fine insectproof mesh until they are 7–10cm (2¾–4in) tall and keep plants well watered during dry periods. Starting off brassica seedlings in modules under cover and then transplanting them once they have four to five true leaves is also recommended.

❝ ❞

CONDUCTING A PLANT HEALTH CHECK (SEE P130) IS THE FIRST LINE OF DEFENCE WHEN IT COMES TO PEST CONTROL.

As seedlings develop, they are better able to withstand flea-beetle damage, which will have little, if any, impact on the harvest.

C. Carrot fly
The destructive larvae of carrot fly bore holes into carrot roots and the damage is visible only when you pull them up. There are two preventative measures you can take and the easiest is to choose carrot-root fly resistant varieties such as 'Flyaway'. The second option is to use fine insectproof mesh and erect a 2ft-(60cm-) high enclosure around the crop when seedlings appear. This makes the carrot inaccessible to the low-flying insects.

D. Cabbage root fly
The maggots (larvae) of the cabbage root fly feed on brassica roots and can easily kill young plants. An effective and free DIY solution is to make rubber "collars" out of old wellies. The collars prevent adult female cabbage root flies from laying eggs at the base of the stem. Cut old wellies into circles around 15–20cm (6–8in) in diameter, make a slit from edge to centre, then cut a small hole in the middle for the stem. When you transplant brassica seedlings, simply place the collar around the base of the stem. Alternatively you can bulk-buy brassica collars.

E. Allium leaf miner
Tunnelling through the leaves, stems, and bulbs of alliums, allium leaf miner maggots severely damage plants, which leaves them vulnerable to diseases, especially rot. The only preventative measure is to cover allium crops with insect-proof mesh during periods when the female flies are looking for plants to lay eggs on. This happens in early spring and again in autumn.

TIP

CROP ROTATION IS STRONGLY RECOMMENDED IF YOU DISCOVER DAMAGE FROM CARROT FLY, CABBAGE ROOT FLY, OR ALLIUM LEAF MINER.

Rubber collars fitted around young kale plants protect them from the destructive cabbage root fly.

F. Cabbage whites

There are two types of cabbage white butterflies. Large cabbage whites lay batches of eggs that turn into yellow and green caterpillars with black dots, while small cabbage whites tend to lay individual eggs and the caterpillars are pale green. You can choose to grow brassicas under insectproof mesh, but ensure the leaves don't touch the material or the butterflies will simply lay their eggs through it. My preferred option is to regularly check my brassica plants, squishing eggs and removing caterpillars when I see them. It seems to be working because cabbage whites are causing less damage year on year.

G. Mice and voles

These small, hungry mammals can wreak havoc by nibbling young seedlings, especially those raised under cover, and eating recently sown legume seeds. They have a talent for finding the seeds, whether in modules or in raised beds. When I sow peas and beans in modules, I put the trays on the top two levels of my greenhouse shelves to make them as inaccessible as possible to these clever creatures. In particularly bad years, they have nibbled the tops off seedlings and even damaged pots and fleece. If you feel your mice and vole problem is getting out of hand, the solution is to put down a baited trap of your choice to capture them. My voles and mice are particularly fond of chocolate spread and peanut butter!

H. Slugs and snails

I feel there is too much emphasis on attacking slugs and snails rather than deterring them from accessing your crops in the first place. Use the strategies opposite, which also work against snails, and you'll soon see a decline in your garden's slug population.

Use bramble canes as spiky barriers to protect young seedlings from slugs and snails.

- **Hiding places** Slugs and snails have favourite hiding places – in long grass and under containers, wood, and stones – so one option is to reduce these hiding habitats. Cut grass around the perimeter of beds as short as possible, pick up any stray pieces of wood and large stones, and keep pathways clear.
- **Erecting barriers** Erecting barriers that slugs find difficult to cross can work well. Wool, a fantastic natural product, is an excellent slug deterrent when used as a mulch around plants because the slimy creatures don't like the texture. Fortunately, it is increasingly being used as a protective or insulating material in parcels and packages, so can be sourced from friends, family, and neighbours. Prickly, thorny twigs also make good slug barriers. Lay stems of plants such as gorse and blackberry on the ground around plants as a deterrent. They won't stop every single slug or snail, but will help to reduce damage and are free to source.

- **Time to transplant** Whenever possible, I like to start seedlings off in modules and grow them to a decent size before transplanting. A larger seedling will survive a slug or snail onslaught far more effectively than a small one. Slugs also seem to have a preference for younger seedlings over larger plants.

TIP

LEAVE A FEW LARGE PIECES OF WOOD OR BIG STONES AROUND YOUR PLOT, TURN THEM OVER DAILY AND THEN DISPOSE OF ANY SLUGS OR SNAILS HIDING BENEATH.

DISEASE AND PREVENTION

IDENTIFY PROBLEMS AND IMPROVE PLANTS' RESISTANCE

Although diversity is the best natural defence, disease can enter any growing area. Learn how to spot and deal with the four most common diseases, as well as improve crop resilience and soil health, with homemade preparations.

SOME FORM OF DISEASE IS INEVITABLE EVERY GROWING SEASON SO PLEASE DON'T THINK YOU'RE DOING SOMETHING WRONG!

COMMON DISEASES

Some diseases are simple to deal with, but others, such as blight, can destroy an entire crop if you don't act quickly. Fortunately, the four you are most likely to encounter in the garden are easy to spot and there are prevention and mitigation strategies you can employ.

A. Rust

Appearing as orange-brown patches on foliage, rust tends to affect alliums and broad beans. It won't kill them but reduces photosynthesis, which in turn reduces yields. Simply cut out the worst affected leaves and remove any rusted debris at the end of the season.

B. Powdery mildew

If you spot a powdery, white residue on plant leaves, remove and compost affected foliage right away. This disease spreads quickly in warm, humid weather and can eventually halt growth so keep a close eye on squash, cucurbits, and peas, and apply lactic acid bacteria (LAB/see overleaf).

C. Downy mildew

This fungal disease produces discoloured areas on the upper leaf with grey, white, or purple mould on the underside. It tends to strike brassicas in cool, wet spring weather. Pick off the worst affected leaves and wait for warmer summer temperatures to halt its progress. It also affects squash.

D. Late blight

When it spreads from foliage to fruit, late blight is usually fatal for tomatoes and potatoes. It first appears as dark patches or lesions on stems and leaves so if you spot these signs on potato plants, cut stems to soil level, leave for two to three weeks, and then harvest the crop. For tomatoes, remove an infected plant immediately and always destroy blighted material by burning. Prevent blight by choosing resistant varieties, growing early or second-early potatoes, employing crop rotation, and avoid wetting tomato foliage.

DISEASE PREVENTION

Plants are most susceptible to diseases when just a single crop (a monoculture) is grown in a large area, allowing a particular pathogen to target them and then spread. Pathogens are air- or water-borne microorganisms that transmit disease when environmental conditions allow them to multiply. Growing different plants together in a polyculture, as well as dividing up the same crop and growing it in different sections of your plot (such as courgettes at opposite ends of the garden) is the best way of preventing diseases from taking over or damaging your whole crop. You can also support plant and soil health with excellent natural preparations, such as LAB (below).

Keep clear of chemicals

Spraying plants with synthetic chemicals, such as fungicides to eradicate mildew, simply wipes out the plant's natural forms of defence and increases its dependence on the chemicals. Rainfall then carries the fungicides down into the soil where they can destroy the beneficial microbial life that make nutrients available to plant roots. The unfortunate result can be a reliance on synthetic fertilizers to maintain soil health.

Instead, we can use natural, non-invasive methods of control and prevention, and regard disease as a wider issue arising from a lack of diversity, rather than as a problem to be dealt with in isolation. For example, applying diluted LAB to your crops and soil, combined with growing a wide range of plants, will help keep your garden free from certain disastrous diseases such as powdery mildew and blight.

What is LAB?

The Korean Natural Farming (KNF) method of growing avoids artificial pesticides and fertilizers and relies on naturally occurring microorganisms, such as bacteria and fungi, to strengthen plant growth. One of the best preparations is based on LAB or *lactobacillus*, the "friendly" bacteria found in live yoghurt and probiotic preparations. It works as a kind of biological "emergency service" for plants and soil, as well as an all-round enhancer of the garden environment. It is a fantastic tool for improving soil quality, especially at the start of the season, as it adds beneficial microbial life to depleted soil – as well as to new soil, which needs time to develop a healthy biological balance. LAB also increases plants' resilience to disease.

Making LAB allows us to harvest naturally-occurring *lactobacilli*, and then create a culture (instructions are given overleaf) – a fridge-stable product ready for use throughout the season.

APPLYING REGULAR NATURAL FEEDS TO PLANTS SHOWING THE FIRST SIGNS OF DISEASE CAN INCREASE THEIR DEFENCE MECHANISMS AND SUPPORT RECOVERY.

HOW TO MAKE LAB

The following recipe is adapted from *The Regenerative Grower's Guide to Garden Amendments* by Nigel Palmer.

Ingredients
- 500g (18oz) of uncooked organic white rice
- 1 litre (2 pints) of water (preferably rainwater, borehole water, or spring water – avoid mains water)
- 0.5 litre (1 pint) of best-quality organic cow's or goat's milk (raw or unpasteurized if possible, although any type will work)

Equipment
- Two large mixing bowls
- Two empty 1 litre (2 pint) jar
- Empty 0.5 litre (1 pint) jar
- Piece of cloth and rubber bands
- Pen and labels
- Large sieve

1. Pour the water into one of the mixing bowls and put the rice in the sieve over the second bowl. Start rinsing the rice with the water and collect the run-off. When all the water from the first mixing bowl has been used, swap the bowls around and repeat the rinsing process between five and seven times. You'll notice the water becoming cloudier.

2. After the last rinse, pour the rice water into the 1 litre (2 pint) jar and cover with a piece of cloth, such as muslin. Use a rubber band to hold it in place.

3. Keep the jar of rice water at room temperature (but out of direct sunlight) and leave it for about five days. By now you will see that the rice water has settled into three layers. The top layer is a thin murky-looking film (or scum), the middle layer is clear (and contains the lactic acid bacteria), and the bottom layer is residue.

4. Remove the top layer with a spoon, then pour the clear layer into the second 1 litre (2 pint) jar being careful to leave the residue behind. Dispose of the top and bottom layers on your compost heap. You now have a jar that contains a highly concentrated stock of lactic acid bacteria. This can be stored in the fridge for at least six months and used to make a batch of LAB amendment. Remember to label the jar and include the date it was made.

5. To prepare the LAB for use in the garden, mix the stock with the organic milk in a 1 litre (2 pint) jar using a 1:10 ratio of stock to milk. Stir both ingredients together thoroughly. Then, as before, place a cloth over the lid of the jar, secure it with a rubber band, and store at room temperature out of direct sunlight for a week.

6. After a week the contents of the jar will have settled into three layers. Remove the curds (top layer) so you're left with a liquid (the whey). Line the sieve with muslin, set it over a bowl, then carefully strain the whey, leaving the sediment behind.

7. Pour the strained liquid into a 0.5 litre (1 pint) jar, label, date, and store in a fridge for up to two weeks. The curds and sediment can be composted.

TIP

WHEN YOU'VE CREATED NEW RAISED BEDS AND FILLED THEM, ADD LAB TO THE SOIL TO GIVE IT A FANTASTIC BOOST AND GET YOUR PLANTS OFF TO A HEALTHY START.

The jar of LAB has separated into curds and liquid whey.

LAB IN ACTION

This highly concentrated resource must be very well diluted for garden use. Add roughly two teaspoons of LAB per standard watering can holding 10 litres (17½ pints) of water. Below are some recommend uses for diluted LAB.

Soil improver

LAB helps to break down organic matter into nutrients that are readily absorbed by plants, and it also stimulates microbiological processes in the soil. When plants have access to more nutrients, they are healthier, produce greater yields, and have a much greater resilience to certain pests and diseases. If you are starting a new growing season or have a new raised bed, water the soil with diluted LAB once a week for the first few weeks to improve soil quality.

Compost accelerator

LAB helps stimulate biological activity. On a dry day, water new or incomplete compost piles with 10 litres (17½ pints) of double strength diluted LAB (2ml per 1 litre/⅓tsp

to 2 pints of water) to encourage microbial activity. If using the chicken composting system (see pp58–61), try watering the piles with diluted LAB on a weekly basis to accelerate decomposition.

Plant booster

Once a week to once a fortnight, water young plants with diluted LAB to maintain levels of beneficial bacteria around their roots and stems. These organisms help to improve nutrient uptake and their high numbers ward off any pathogens, often by out-competing them.

Foliar spray

For the first few weeks in the life of seedlings, while the root systems are still developing, spray diluted LAB onto the leaves to protect against disease. Alternatively, when you spot the first signs of disease, such as powdery mildew, generously spray the whole crop with diluted LAB. The bacteria will begin to colonize the leaves, helping to prevent the pathogen from taking hold.

TIP

IT AMAZES ME HOW MUCH FASTER COMPOST MATERIAL BREAKS DOWN ONCE LAB IS APPLIED.

Regular spraying with diluted LAB is a fantastic way to support and boost the health of my young plants.

MULCHES

MATERIALS TO SPREAD AROUND YOUR PLANTS

Mulching offers many benefits from retaining moisture to restricting weed growth. Homemade compost is the mulch I use most often because it improves the soil, but I've also discovered some fantastic alternatives.

TIP

WHEN YOU SEE TREES BEING PROFESSIONALLY PRUNED, ASK TREE SURGEONS FOR A FEW BAGS OF WOODCHIP. THEY ARE USUALLY HAPPY TO OBLIGE – FOR FREE OR FOR A SMALL DONATION.

Of all the materials used for mulching, from manure to grass cuttings, compost is the most versatile. Homemade compost encourages beneficial soil microbes and fungi that in turn boost plant health, making them less vulnerable to pests and diseases. As a bonus, it is less attractive to slugs than other mulches, so it will help to keep your slug population under control. I've also had great results with the following three materials.

Woodchip

Perennials need soil fungi to thrive and woodchip, which promotes fungal growth, makes an excellent mulch for them. Woodchip is often considered a waste resource so it's great to find a use for it. Breaking down slowly over time, woodchip provides a slow release of nutrients and also soaks up water like a sponge. It is the ideal mulching material during dry weather.

I mulch my strawberries with woodchip (it keeps the fruit clean), as well as my soft fruit and perennial herbs. In spring, spread a layer of woodchip at least 5cm (2in) deep around the base of plants and repeat on an annual basis. When using any mulching material it's vital to leave a little space between the mulch and the plant stem to allow air to circulate. This avoids potential issues such as rot and disease. I wouldn't recommend using fresh woodchip as a mulch and suggest you heap it up and allow the pile to break down for around 9 to 12 months before applying.

Stones

Mulching around plants with stones may strike you as odd but their dense structure effectively captures the sun's energy. A layer of stones works as a "heat sink", warming the ground to create microclimates within your garden. When growing heat-loving crops such as tomatoes, peppers, and pumpkins, place stones around the base of seedlings to help them develop. Slabs of slate or slate chippings work particularly well because their dark colour captures a lot of heat. A stone or slate mulch will also reduce moisture loss from the soil.

Wool

One of our most incredible natural resources, wool is, to my mind, underused, but we can give it a new lease of life in the garden. Employed as a mulch it will not only conserve moisture but, as a bonus, also deter slugs. Wool is also easily sourced from packaging material.

I first got this idea from no-dig gardener Adam Jones, who had spread packaging wool over his brassica bed with fantastic results. Although the bed bordered a dark hedge with plenty of long grass (the perfect slug habitat), there wasn't a single sign of slug damage. The creatures clearly find it difficult to travel over wool with its coarse, dry texture. Please encourage your family, friends, and neighbours to save their wool packaging then spread it around brassicas and annual salads.

Strawberries mulched with one-year-old woodchip (*right*), heat-retaining slate around a spaghetti squash plant (*below*), and spreading a wool mulch beneath kale plants (*below right*).

TIP

IF REQUESTS FOR WOOL FROM PACKAGING AND PARCELS RESULT IN A BIG INFLUX OF MATERIAL, JUST PUT ANY EXCESS ON YOUR COMPOST HEAP.

FROST PROTECTION

HOW TO SAFEGUARD TENDER PLANTS

Like most gardeners, I'm impatient to start sowing when spring arrives but starting off too many tender crops too early means constantly worrying about frost protection. Below are my suggestions for early harvests without disasters.

I tend to start sowing most of my tender crops about four weeks before the last average frost date for my growing zone, which reduces time spent protecting plants and bringing in seedlings overnight. Below I have outlined a few strategies I employ to protect plants against frost if it's forecast.

WATER EARLY

A simple but lesser-known strategy to reduce frost damage is to water your plants the morning before an overnight frost is expected. This gives the soil enough time to warm up and because moist soil holds heat better than dry, your plants will be better protected through the night.

CLOCHES

Individual plants such as a tender herb, a courgette, or a sweet pepper, can be protected with glass cloches when frost is forecast. The best time to cover them is early afternoon so the plant sits in a mini-greenhouse in warm soil. It's also worth watering a plant before placing a cloche over it, for the reasons given above.

Glass cloches are expensive but an upturned cardboard box lined with an insulating material such as wool or thick fabric is a great alternative. This creates a "warm room" that will retain heat overnight and keep seedlings protected. Always weigh down the box with stones or wood so it doesn't get blown away in the wind.

FLEECE ALTERNATIVES

Currently, the most popular frost protection for home growers is horticultural fleece but I'm gradually phasing it out owing to the plastic microfibre content. Environmentally friendly alternatives that can be sourced at low cost or for free include old rags, bedsheets, and my favourite fleece substitute – hessian. This fantastic natural product is made from plant fibres and has excellent insulating properties, as evidenced by its use in the building trade to protect newly laid bricks from frost damage.

I usually add one extra layer of hessian for every potential drop of 2°C. For example, if I am expecting a frost of -1 to -2°C, one layer is fine but if the temperature is forecast to drop to -3°C or -4°C I add another layer over the first. If you are using old sheeting or another fabric that is thinner than hessian, add another layer or two.

TIP

NATURAL, BIODEGRADABLE HESSIAN IS WIDELY AVAILABLE FROM BUILDERS' MERCHANTS. A LARGE ROLL WILL LAST YOU FOR YEARS.

Frosts can also strike late in the season. When an autumn frost is forecast I protect my dwarf beans using hessian to extend their cropping period.

MAKE A PROTECTIVE STRUCTURE

**When frost is forecast make this simple tent to trap warm air
and insulate tender or half-hardy plants.**

1. Gather together some tall sticks of roughly equal height (45–50cm/18–20in) and push them just under halfway down into the ground around the plants so they're stable.
2. Place small, upturned pots over the ends of the sticks to stop the fabric ripping.

3. Drape hessian or sheeting over the sticks and pots, ensuring the fabric is held well away from the leaves. The best time to do this is mid- to late afternoon to retain some warmth. Remove the hessian or sheeting the following morning to allow light in.

PLANTS TO PROTECT

The five crops below can all benefit from the insulation offered by the structure:
° Potatoes (tender)
° Dwarf beans (tender)
° Fennel (half-hardy)
° Squash (tender)
° Young carrot seedlings (to prevent shock)

On this frosty morning in mid-autumn, the hardy crops need no protection, but I'd already covered the tender leaves in the salad bed with fleece the day before.

THE YEARLY SERVICE

JUST LIKE A CAR, A GARDEN NEEDS TO BE MAINTAINED

A well-run garden that receives regular care and attention tends to have fewer problems. I'll show you how to effectively service your garden so you can enjoy the spring and summer months disaster-free (hopefully!).

A WELL-CARED-FOR GARDEN WILL SAVE YOU A LOT OF TIME AND MONEY IN THE LONG RUN.

A couple of years ago, it was time to start the spring sowings. However, over winter, the old compost bins had completely fallen apart so I had to dismantle them and then build new bins ready for the season ahead. The timing was very inconvenient, but compost is the currency of the garden, so I placed the sowing on hold to fix the issue. Had I adequately inspected the compost bins the autumn before and made a note of their condition, I would have had plenty of time to rectify the problem before the new season started. From that experience, the idea of the yearly service was born and I'd like to share with you how we can anticipate and prevent problems in the garden.

CARRYING OUT THE SERVICE

The aim of the yearly service is to find the most pressing potential issues and finding time to sort them before the new season. I recommend carrying out a check every autumn to allow plenty of time to save up, source materials, and make any necessary repairs in time for spring. Mid-autumn is the ideal time, when the garden is fairly bare and it's easier to assess the situation.

Take a notepad, pen, and a hot drink and head up to the garden. Aim to spend a whole morning conducting a service. Slowly walk around your garden, starting at the boundaries then working inwards, and thoroughly inspect everything. It is vital to address such issues as wobbly fence posts immediately because the problem will only get worse. Note down any problems so you can work on a solution.

QUESTIONS TO ASK YOURSELF

A doctor usually asks a patient about their symptoms to diagnose the problem, and you can use the same approach to identify potential issues in key areas, for example:
- How much compost is ready?
- Do I need more pots or modules?
- Are there any rips in the polytunnel?
- Do any tools need oiling?
- Are there any holes in the fences?
- Is the shed gutter clear of plant debris?

Carrying out the yearly service also has a hidden benefit. Building on the Observe and Interact method (see pp34–37), it offers a similar opportunity to take a fresh look at your garden as a whole and see more potential in the space. Fired up by this knowledge you can make more accurate and exciting plans for the coming season.

Around two to three weeks before the spring growing season gets underway and I've completed all the jobs on my list, there is one more maintenance task. I like to take one final look at the water infrastructure to check that the cold weather over winter hasn't cracked any pipes.

Check key structures and equipment are in top condition. Assess your irrigation system (*top*), survey boundaries (*below left*), and check that plant supports are in good shape (*below right*).

PRODUCTIVITY
TECHNIQUES

Make the most out of your growing space and enjoy your biggest harvest yet

SUCCESSION PLANTING

STRATEGIES FOR CONTINUOUS CROPS

Sowing or planting crops in succession is an invaluable technique for increasing the productivity of your growing space. Both approaches – simple and staggered – are very easy ways to increase yields and extend cropping.

TIP

FLORENCE FENNEL SITS IN THE GROUND WELL FROM LATE SUMMER TO MID-AUTUMN, SO I ALWAYS ADD A FEW EXTRA SEEDS WHEN I MAKE THE FINAL SOWING IN EARLY SUMMER.

Using simple succession planting, a new crop immediately replaces one that has been harvested. This entails planning ahead so you have seedlings ready to plant in the cleared space. Staggered succession sowing allows you to spread harvests over a longer period. Both these approaches are designed to maximize productivity over the growing season and are key to the success of the monthly planting plan (see pp160–163), which I introduce later in the chapter. For now, I'd like to focus on the benefits of staggered succession sowing.

SOW IN BATCHES

To minimize gluts – root vegetables are common culprits – try sowing seeds of a single crop in batches. The master growing chart on pages 94–99 is your guide and will show you the sowing "window" for each crop.

The window for beetroot in growing zone 8 (see p97), for example, is between March and June and sowing a couple of rows once a month over this period will produce harvests from June right through to December. Some vegetables, such as garlic, have a limited sowing window while others, such as tomatoes, crop for an extended period and sowing in stages isn't appropriate. I would also suggest avoiding staggered sowings of winter crops that need as much late-season light and warmth as possible to mature.

SALADS AND ANNUAL HERBS

Crops such as lettuce, rocket, and coriander are prone to bolting in the hot weather and you lose harvests. Sowing a new batch of

salad crops and annual herbs every couple of weeks throughout spring and early summer will result in better yields, especially if you start them off in modules. Compost the oldest plants and replace these with new seedlings right away. Don't forget to grow salads in partial shade and keep them well watered in dry weather to prolong their cropping period.

EIGHT CROPS FOR SUCCESSION SOWING
Peas

Sow a new batch every couple of weeks between early spring (under cover) and then direct from mid-spring until early summer for continuous cropping throughout summer and early autumn. If you have a polytunnel or greenhouse, start peas a month earlier than usual and grow them up a trellis for an early crop before outdoor peas are ready.

Dwarf beans

These unsung heroes are perfect for small spaces and make excellent gap-fillers. Start a tray of dwarf French beans under cover every couple of weeks between mid-spring and early summer.

Broad beans

Sow a batch of broad beans (or field beans) direct every two to three weeks from late winter to late spring for harvests into early autumn.

Turnips

Direct sow a new row every couple of weeks throughout spring and summer.

Kohlrabi

Start off a new batch in modules every month throughout spring and summer. Purple varieties are recommended for autumn and early winter crops because they are hardier than the green types.

Potatoes

Potatoes are straightforward to succession plant: just follow the timings given for earlies, seconds, and maincrop varieties (see p97). Planting blight-resistant varieties, such as 'Sarpo Mira', will allow you to harvest outdoor-grown potatoes in autumn.

Florence fennel

I like to start off 15–20 seedlings every two to three weeks in modules between mid-spring and early summer for a gradual but consistent harvest.

Carrots

Sow direct throughout spring. Harvest early varieties in summer but leave longer-maturing varieties in the ground through to winter.

Sowing the last row of carrots after harvesting an early maturing variety.

TIP

IF YOU HAVE A POLYTUNNEL, TRY SUCCESSION SOWING CARROTS FROM LATE WINTER. SOW ONE ROW EVERY TWO WEEKS UNTIL EARLY SPRING FOR EARLIER HARVESTS THAN OUTDOOR CARROTS.

POLYCULTURE

MAINTAIN VARIETY IN THE VEG GARDEN

Growing different plants together imitates the biodiversity in nature and gives a more organic feel to a growing space. Polyculture is a fantastic tool for garden design, improves soil, and protects plants from pests and diseases.

TIP

IF YOU ARE NEW TO POLYCULTURE, THE BEST PLACE TO START IS BY SOWING A VARIETY OF SALAD CROPS.

POLYCULTURE PLANTING
Practising polyculture means growing two or more types of plants together, rather than cultivating a single crop in rows or blocks. While I opt for standard planting for crops such as brassicas and potatoes, I firmly believe that polyculture can make a positive difference in the right conditions. The following groups of plants will all thrive when planted in a polyculture.

Salads
Radish, spinach, lettuce, oriental greens, peas and broad beans (for shoots), chard, spring onions, and any other salad staple, all work well planted together. The spacings between each plant are similar, which makes it easy to mix the crops and create a beautiful and productive polyculture.

Herbs
Creating a small collection of your favourite annual herbs is a fantastic way to establish a polyculture. Grow them at the end of one of your raised beds or in a large container, and try adding an unusual herb such as chervil.

A mix of perennial herbs grown in a raised bed also works well, as long as you plant herbs that prefer drier conditions around the edges. Put those that prefer more moisture in the middle and hand water only these plants. The other herbs will be much happier with just rainfall.

Annual flowers
Choose four or five annual flowers with different but complementary growing habits to create a stunning border. A combination of tall sunflowers, bushy cosmos, and sprawling nasturtiums would work really well. Or simply use them to add splashes of colour to a small space. You can also combine flowers with herbs to create beautiful islands of colour and scent in the vegetable garden (see pp186–199).

Root vegetables with alliums
Planting carrots with onions and shallots is a fantastic way of deterring carrot fly because the alliums mask the scent of the carrots and the fly can't locate them. Growing beetroot and turnips with alliums also works well and the young root vegetable leaves are also edible, giving you more harvests from the same space.

Fellow permaculturist and author of *Edible Paradise*, Vera Greutink, has inspired me hugely. She takes her polycultures to the next level by creating themed plantings such as "pizza" and "Mexican". Why not try and create your own themed polyculture bed, perhaps one that's inspired by your gin collection or love of pasta?

Planted at the end of my raised vegetable beds, fennel and borage (*front left*) are insect magnets while sweet peas (*middle*) add welcome colour and scent.

INTERCROPPING IDEAS

Also known as interplanting, this form of polyculture is based around two to four different crops that are grown together in a fairly uniform style. The goal is to grow as much food as possible using every inch of space available, which is especially important for small-space growing. The secret of success with intercropping is to try out different combinations so you find one that suits your goals and needs. Here are seven ideas to try so you can see just how effective intercropping can be:

- Runner beans with spinach, parsley, or coriander
- Onions with radish, carrots, or lettuce
- Tomatoes with basil
- Sweetcorn with dwarf peas, nasturtiums, or cucumbers
- Kale with turnips
- Fennel with spinach
- Cucumbers with calendula or nasturtiums

Be aware that intercropping isn't the best option for all vegetable types when aiming for maximum productivity. For example, I grow garlic so closely together that there isn't space for anything else, and the last thing you want to do is smother plants as this can reduce the yields.

The three sisters

This combination of three crops is perhaps the best-known example of intercropping to maximize production. The climbing beans grow up the sweetcorn, which acts as natural support, and the squash expands over the ground, creating a living mulch that keeps the roots of the sweetcorn and beans moist.

Growing direct-sown carrots between onions started from sets helps deter carrot flies.

RELAY CROPPING

This lesser-known growing method combines intercropping with succession planting and allows you to extend your growing season by a few weeks – a huge bonus in cooler climates. Once a crop is getting close to maturity (usually two to six weeks from harvesting) you sow the next inbetween the plants that are still standing.

My preference is to direct sow between a mature crop around two to four weeks before harvesting, which gives the seeds time to germinate and start developing a strong root system. As soon as the original crop is harvested, the next is ready to take over. Relay cropping is also a fantastic way to increase soil health by keeping the surface covered and maintaining living roots in the ground.

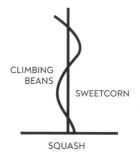

This simple graphic shows how the three "sister" crops combine to maximize space.

CLIMBING BEANS

SWEETCORN

SQUASH

The tomatoes in this raised bed can be interplanted with basil grown in plugs.

> **TIP**
>
> FROM LATE SUMMER, UNDERPLANT TOMATOES WITH WINTER SALADS – BY THE TIME THE TOMATO PLANTS ARE REMOVED THE SALADS WILL BE NEARLY READY FOR HARVESTING.

THE HUNGRY GAP

KEY CROPS TO SEE YOU THROUGH

Between early spring and early summer there is limited homegrown produce available in the UK and other temperate climates. The so-called hungry gap comes before summer crops are ready, but with forethought you can still harvest food.

TIP

ANOTHER FANTASTIC CROP FOR THE HUNGRY GAP IS SPAGHETTI SQUASH. HARVEST IN SEPTEMBER THEN STORE IN A COOL, DARK, DRY PLACE UNTIL EARLY SUMMER THE FOLLOWING YEAR!

The lean period at the end of the winter-vegetable season is without doubt one of the most challenging times of the year for home growers because we find ourselves with little on offer compared to the abundance of summer, autumn, and winter. To ensure you have fresh produce to harvest requires advance planning, including sowing some crops, such as kale, the previous spring and leaving them to overwinter. The monthly plan (see overleaf) is your go-to tool for timings. Also, if you have the space, try dedicating a raised bed to growing crops for the hungry gap then using interplanting methods to get summer and autumn harvests from the same space. Here are five versatile crops you can harvest during this period.

A. Kale
Although kale is primarily known for its leaves, the real magic of this crop comes during the hungry gap when you can and harvest the flower stems in spring. An excellent purple sprouting broccoli alternative, the stem can be enjoyed raw, roasted, steamed, boiled, or charred.

B. Purple sprouting broccoli
Abundant throughout spring, purple sprouting broccoli produces a forest of delicious, sweet, purple spears. The leaves are also edible, but cook them before eating. Sow "early purple sprouting" varieties that will crop the following spring – in time to eat during the hungry gap.

C. Rhubarb
This easy-to-grow perennial can be harvested from early spring until the start of summer. Stewed to make desserts and sweet preserves, rhubarb is also good in savoury dishes. The strained liquid can be used as a sustainable alternative to lemon juice.

D. Spring cabbage
Eaten on its own, cabbage is a little bland, but there are many simple ways to elevate this longstanding staple into something more appealing. Try cutting it into wedges, then covering with a spice mix and roasting, or make your own kimchi. Harvest from the end of winter.

E. Wild garlic
This is my favourite crop during the hungry gap and, once established, wild garlic will provide plentiful harvests every spring. Buy seeds or bulbs and plant them in a shady or partially shady spot, but be patient: your wild-garlic patch will need a couple of years to develop. The fresh leaves are delicious: try them in a wild-garlic salsa verde.

- **Potatoes** Start off early potatoes in a greenhouse in late winter to keep them protected from frosts. Expect to enjoy your first new potatoes by mid-spring.
- **Nettles** Harvest young plants from spring to use as a nutritious spinach substitute.
- **Broad beans** Sow under cover in trays in late winter, then pick and eat the delicious shoots when they are around 10cm (4in) tall.
- **Lettuce, spinach, and, radish** Start off under cover in pots in late winter. In early spring, move into a coldframe or plant out under a cloche for harvests from mid-spring onwards.
- **Swiss chard** Leave to overwinter and they will send up a flourish of welcome, fresh-green growth during spring.

THE MONTHLY PLANTING PLAN

THE BEST WAY TO STAY ORGANIZED

Timing and forward planning are key to growing food in abundance and in recent years I've embraced the monthly planting plan, which I'd like to share. It has massively improved the productivity and efficiency of my garden.

"

MY CORE GOAL WHEN CREATING THE MONTHLY PLANTING PLAN WAS TO IMPROVE THE EFFICIENCY OF SUCCESSION PLANTING IN THE GARDEN.

WHY ADOPT A MONTHLY PLAN?
In traditional planting plans, an entire growing year tends to get crammed onto a single sheet of paper, but the monthly plan splits the year into 12 months, each with its own detailed overview. First, let's look at some of the many benefits you can expect from creating your own plan, then I'll explain in detail how to draw it up.

Information at a glance
The monthly plan has enough space for noting down key harvests, sowings, and transplantings, making it easy to get an instant overview, as well as a sense of the month ahead. Used alongside the master growing chart (see pp94–99), it makes the perfect planning tool.

Help with timing
I found distinguishing between the months on a traditional yearly plan fairly difficult and realized I was letting certain tasks slip. With the monthly plan, I found it much easier to keep focused on the month in hand, complete tasks in a timely manner, and keep on track.

Filling gaps
When you work through the plan month by month, it's easy to look ahead and predict when a gap may appear. It acts as a reminder to start off crops in modules a month or two earlier so you'll have something to fill that space.

Smooth transition
One of the trickiest elements when creating a traditional planting plan from scratch is working around crops from last year that are still in the ground. With the monthly plan you simply continue straight into the next growing year, incorporating crops from the previous season into the upcoming one. It makes planning straightforward as well as much less stressful.

Valuable data
Any planting plan is a useful resource for future growing seasons, enabling you to assess what did and didn't work and helping to influence the way you continue to use the growing area. I found the monthly plan particularly helpful in understanding how much space a particular crop took up so I could decide whether I wanted to grow more or less of it next year.

CREATING THE PLAN

Follow the sequence below and you'll find it's a simple way to
map out your growing space and plan for the year ahead.

1. DRAW THE MASTER TEMPLATE

A bird's-eye view of your growing space will
be the master template for each month – I've
included an example template (below) for
reference. Once you've completed the
template, either drawing it by hand or
creating it digitally, you need to make 12
copies – one for each month. Always leave
enough space to one side for the name of
the month, plus boxes to act as checklists or
to explain abbreviations. I use the following
three boxes on my template:

- **Key module/succession sowings** crops to
  sow in modules now for transplanting later
- **Key transplantings** crops to be planted
  out this month
- **Key direct sowings** crops to be direct sown
  this month

Abbreviations

I allocate tasks to different times of
the month to help spread the workload.
E, M, and L on my plan (overleaf) signify early,
mid-month, and late.

2. CHOOSE YOUR STAPLES

Next, make a list of up to 12 staples – your
must-grow crops that are productive, tasty,
and versatile. I aim for a maximum of 60–70%
of the total garden area to be given over to
staples so I can grow other crops. Also make
a note of follow-on staples for succession
planting later in the season. Here is my list
of staples:

- beetroot
- broad beans
- carrots
- garlic
- kale
- leeks
- onions
- peas
- potatoes
- purple sprouting broccoli
- runner beans
- winter cabbage

TIP

FOR SIMPLICITY,
DEDICATE A
WHOLE OR PART
OF A BED TO
ANNUAL HERBS AND
SALADS THAT YOU
CAN PLANT
IN SUCCESSION
THROUGHOUT THE
GROWING SEASON.

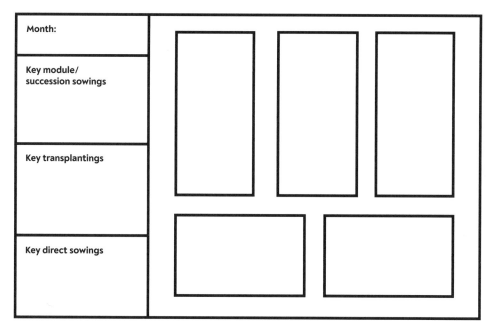

Month:
Key module/ succession sowings
Key transplantings
Key direct sowings

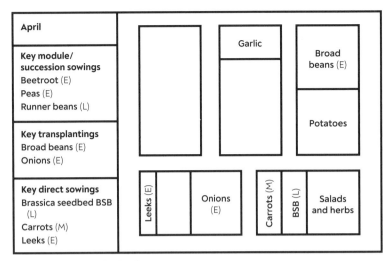

April

Key module/ succession sowings
Beetroot (E)
Peas (E)
Runner beans (L)

Key transplantings
Broad beans (E)
Onions (E)

Key direct sowings
Brassica seedbed BSB (L)
Carrots (M)
Leeks (E)

Garlic

Broad beans (E)

Potatoes

Leeks (E)

Onions (E)

Carrots (M)

BSB (L)

Salads and herbs

Staples (in bold) are filled in first to help me plan out the rest of the growing season.

3. ADD STAPLES TO THE PLAN

Make 12 copies of your master template and label one for each month. Starting with either February or March, consult your master growing chart and choose areas for your staple crops, dividing up raised beds if you're growing multiple crops in one space. Decide how much space to allocate to each crop and don't fill more than 70 per cent with staples.

Fill in the boxes for each month, then add the relevant staple crops in their growing spaces – I recomend highlighting these in some way, by colour for example, to distinguish them from non-staple crops. Once a month is complete, I copy the locations of last month's crops onto next month's sheet, update the boxes with new tasks, and add the new crops. The boxes will guide you through the season and help you to fill in the bird's-eye view of your space.

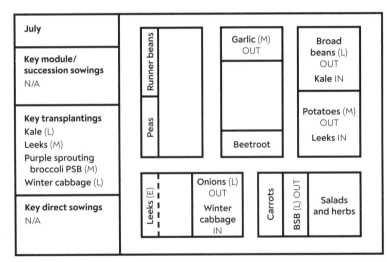

July

Key module/ succession sowings
N/A

Key transplantings
Kale (L)
Leeks (M)
Purple sprouting broccoli PSB (M)
Winter cabbage (L)

Key direct sowings
N/A

Runner beans

Peas

Garlic (M)
OUT

Beetroot

Broad beans (L)
OUT
Kale IN

Potatoes (M)
OUT
Leeks IN

Leeks (E)

Onions (L)
OUT
Winter cabbage
IN

Carrots

BSB (L) OUT

Salads and herbs

July is a month of transition when staples are harvested (OUT) and replaced (IN) by follow-on staples.

4. INPUT FOLLOW-ON STAPLES

By referring back to previous months and using the master growing chart, you can work out when a staple crop can be harvested so you can succession plant a crop in its place. This might be in July when potatoes or broad beans are ready and can be replaced with other staples such as kale or leeks. On my plan, I look through the months and use OUT and IN to signify a change of crop and dotted lines to show previous crop boundaries when the new planting takes up more or less space. Then I go back and check I've made a note in earlier months to start off the crops for transplanting.

5. FILL IN THE WHOLE PLAN

Once you have your 12 staples planned for the 12 months, fill up the rest of the plan with all the other crops you want to grow. In the boxes at the side, I recommend adding lots of handy reminders as well as crop lists.

Producing your own monthly plan is a great opportunity to be creative and have fun with a design that is unique to you and your space. Also, remember that you can always use interplanting to fit in extra harvests between or around your main crops.

TRANSITIONING TO NEXT SEASON

At the end of each growing season, go through your monthly plan and note down any changes you want to make, such as growing more peas. Then, using the past growing season to calculate how much space each crop occupies, create another 12 copies from the master template and continue the process into the new season. Don't forget to work around any staple crops that may still be in the ground, such as garlic, and base the plan around your 12 (or fewer) core staples.

Creating your first monthly plan is a fairly steep learning curve, but the time and effort you invest will be well worth it in the long run. Consult the Resources section (p216) for more information about creating and using the monthly planting plan.

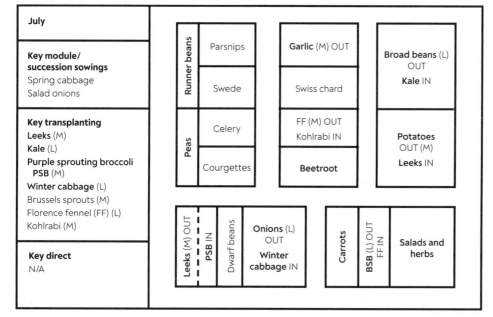

July

Key module/ succession sowings
Spring cabbage
Salad onions

Key transplanting
Leeks (M)
Kale (L)
Purple sprouting broccoli
  PSB (M)
Winter cabbage (L)
Brussels sprouts (M)
Florence fennel (FF) (L)
Kohlrabi (M)

Key direct
N/A

Runner beans — Parsnips / Swede
Peas — Celery / Courgettes

Garlic (M) OUT
Swiss chard
FF (M) OUT
Kohlrabi IN
Beetroot

Broad beans (L) OUT
Kale IN
Potatoes OUT (M)
Leeks IN

Leeks (M) OUT / PSB IN
Dwarf beans
Onions (L) OUT
Winter cabbage IN

Carrots
BSB (L) OUT / FF IN
Salads and herbs

When non-staples for July are added, the monthly plan gives me a level of detail that would be impossible to fit onto a single-sheet plan for the whole year.

TIP

CHECK WHAT IS READY FOR TRANSPLANTING FROM ANY MODULE SOWINGS MADE THE PREVIOUS MONTH BEFORE YOU FILL IN THE CROPS ON THE NEXT MONTHLY PLAN.

Winter is a great time to make changes. I'm reconfiguring the layout to increase the growing area and will adapt my monthly planting plan accordingly.

WORKING WITH SHADE

MAKING THE MOST OF LESS-SUNNY SPOTS

Every garden has a dark corner or shady area and finding the best use for it can be a challenge. I'd like to share my strategies for dealing with shade as well as suggesting some shade-tolerant crops.

DON'T BE AFRAID TO PUSH THE BOUNDARIES WHEN IT COMES TO GROWING PLANTS IN SHADE. THE RESULTS WILL OFTEN SURPRISE YOU.

What to do with a shady corner may be an ongoing issue for gardeners with large plots, but it is a more pressing issue for those aiming to maximize food production in a limited space. Here are four suggestions for turning shady areas in both small and large gardens to your advantage.

Compost
The best use of a shady area in a small garden is a compost setup. Compost bins don't need direct sunlight for their contents to break down effectively and positioning them in sun is a waste of prime growing space. A shady spot is also ideal for piles of mulching materials, such as woodchip and leaf mould, that need to be left for a year or two to break down fully.

Water storage
Shady spots next to a roof are perfect for capturing rainwater, either in butts or water tanks. Direct light heats up the temperature of the water and also encourages algae growth but water stored out of the sun stays cooler, fresher, and algae-free for longer. If your shady spot is far from a source of water but the ground slopes down towards it, consider having a pipe installed to feed a water tank.

Leafy greens
When planning to grow food in a shady spot, the first thing I do is look up to make sure there is a clear patch of blue (or grey) sky above it (even tolerant plants still need some sunlight). If no overhanging branches are blocking the light then I'm happy to try growing a few of the more shade-tolerant crops listed opposite to see how they fare. I always take instructions regarding the site and sunlight requirements of plants with a pinch of salt, so don't be afraid to push against the conventional words of wisdom and experiment a little yourself. The only downside is that your harvests may be smaller.

Poultry
A shady corner is also a great place for housing poultry because the birds will appreciate cooler conditions in summer. Quail are a fantastic option for smaller spaces, while ducks and chickens can be kept in larger areas providing there is a sunny spot connected to the poultry run that the birds can bask in during good weather. Keeping poultry in a shady area works in tandem with a chicken compost system (see pp58–61) to create a fantastic source of fertile and organic matter for the rest of your garden.

Harvesting lettuce grown in a part of the garden that only gets an hour of summer sunshine a day!

10 GREAT CROPS FOR SHADY SPOTS

Test out a few of the crops listed in your shady corners to see which are most successful.

- Lettuce
- Spinach
- Beans and peas (for shoots)
- Kale
- Cabbage
- Parsley
- Coriander
- Swiss chard
- Jerusalem artichokes
- Rhubarb

TOWARDS SELF-SUFFICIENCY

A PART-TIME, SEASONAL APPROACH

Growing all your own food is an admirable goal but such an ambitious target is best approached in stages. My recommendation is to adopt a simple strategy that I call "part-time sufficiency" to help you on your journey.

To many people, self-sufficiency means growing absolutely everything you need, such as enough potatoes to last you an entire year. I take a less-extreme view and suggest you proceed on a temporary or part-time basis then build on this experience to reach your long-term goal. In practice this means growing enough of a particular crop to last a certain period of time, such as salad leaves for harvesting outdoors from spring through to autumn.

VERSATILE CROPS

The following five, easy-to-grow crops are all highly suitable for the part-time sufficiency approach.

Cut and come again salads

A 1.2m x 1.2m (4ft x 4ft) raised bed will easily yield enough salad for two people from spring to mid-autumn. Sow a new row every couple of weeks to maintain a constant supply and cover with a layer of fleece or hessian when frost threatens to extend the growing season (see p144).

Kale

With good planning you can pick the leaves of this remarkably hardy crop year round, then eat the flowering shoots the following spring.

Onions

Given space, it is possible to grow enough onions to last through autumn and winter if stored in a cool, dry place.

Potatoes

Grow them in large 25–30 litre (5½–6½ gallon) containers so you have more space in your beds for other crops. Enjoy earlies from summer and store maincrop varieties for winter use.

Green herbs

Coriander, dill, and parsley are very productive and easy to grow in pots or at the end of raised beds. Parsley leaves can be harvested and enjoyed fresh throughout the winter and both coriander and dill seeds store well.

DECIDE HOW MUCH TO GROW

Assessing how many plants of a particular crop a household should grow to meet its needs, whether for a few months or a whole year, is virtually impossible because every family and every individual will eat different quantities of the same vegetables. Make a start by trying to calculate your weekly consumption of staples such as onions, potatoes, garlic, carrots, and salad leaves. For example, I use around two bulbs of garlic a week and on that basis I would need to plant 104 cloves for a year's (52 weeks') supply. However, I actually plant a total of 130, which includes an extra 25 per cent in case some fail due to poor germination or pest issues. To work out quantities of crops to last for shorter periods, such as four months, work out how much you eat in a week and adapt the calculation.

When it comes to leafy vegetables, such as kale, working out the optimum number of plants is less straightforward but I find this a fun part of self-sufficiency. When trying to assess how much you might need the following year, look at what you currently grow and base your estimations on that. For example, if 12 kale plants didn't provide quite enough greens to last through the winter, why not grow 16 instead? Also, it's a good idea to experiment with different varieties of crops to discover which perform best in your climate. This not only increases productivity but will also reduce failures (see p174).

CELEBRATE SEASONALITY

True self-sufficiency is about working with the seasons so adjusting what you eat to reflect seasonality is the single biggest step you can take to becoming more self-sufficient. Rather than trying to make your onions last until mid-summer the following year, why not grow leeks to enjoy in the latter stages of winter? You can freeze any surplus and use them until the new batch of onions is ready to harvest.

Preserving crops is one way to be self-sufficient over winter months – for instance, I preserve tomatoes or make sauces that can freeze – however, I prefer to invest my time in growing a diversity of crops for each season. Trying to preserve almost everything you grow in peak season when there is so much to do in the garden is a recipe for burn out. Consider self-sufficiency as "seasonal-sufficiency" and make the most of the bounty in every season, adjusting your meals to reflect what you can pick at its freshest. You may, of course, get bored with certain crops, but why not turn this into an opportunity to get creative and search for new and delicious ways of enjoying them? Growing a wide variety of crops means you can look forward to harvesting something different at every stage of the year and the monthly planting plan on pages 160–163 will help you shape your seasonal harvests to suit your goals.

After harvesting garlic, spread out the bulbs and dry thoroughly in the sun. They will keep for longer.

ARE YOU READY?

If your core reason for gardening is to have fun with time to relax, trying to be completely self-sufficient might not make sense. Becoming self-sufficient requires hard work and careful planning, as well as attention to detail. Setting small challenges and experimenting with part-time sufficiency is, to my mind, the best starting point for most growers. As time progresses, you will gain more experience and discover ways of growing food that best suit your needs and goals.

SMALL-SPACE MINDSET

SPACE-SAVING IDEAS FOR GROWING MORE FOOD

Where space for growing is restricted, productivity is often high because gardeners come up with ingenious ideas for squeezing in as much as possible. This creativity can inspire those of us with larger plots too.

TIP

MAXIMIZE THE PRODUCTIVITY OF YOUR GARDEN BY IMPLEMENTING SPACE-SAVING IDEAS AND STRATEGIES.

I have been to many a patio, small terrace garden, or tiny courtyard and been blown away by the abundance of food growing there. Instead of trying to expand your growing area, try adopting some of these inspiring space-saving methods, as I've done in my own plot. It's a great way to boost productivity. You could also consider splitting the garden up into smaller sections and treating each as an independent mini-garden to maximize yields.

GARDENS WITHIN GARDENS

In larger gardens there will be space to organize raised beds into specific crop groups. For example, bed A could be onions and shallots and bed B potatoes. In terms of efficiency, this works well, especially if you want to maximize yields of a particular crop. Once harvested you can succession plant (see p152) the bed with a different crop.

Techniques such as intercropping and creating a polyculture allow you to fit additional plants around your main crops, for example growing carrots between rows of onions (see pp154–157). You can take this a step further by turning a raised bed into its own standalone garden where different crops are grown together. For the best chance of success, don't cram too many types into the same area but give each a clear theme, such as the edible flower and herb garden, the salad garden, or the winter vegetable garden.

"ODDS AND ENDS" GARDEN

There is always scope for being imaginative when making mini-gardens. An "odds and ends" garden, for example, is a fun idea and simply involves creating a separate place for spare seedlings or random edible plants that you haven't managed to find room for elsewhere. This experimental style of gardening is a great way of discovering new or better ways to grow crops and you can then incorporate your findings into your main planting plan.

FINDING INSPIRATION

I find the best place to look for small-space ideas and inspirational vegetable gardens is online. On Pinterest, for example, when you search for images under very specific terms, such as "raised bed ideas" or "intercropping", you get fantastic results. I've certainly been so inspired by some ideas that I've incorporated or adapted them for my own plot.

When you see something that you think would suit your garden and aligns with your mission statement (see p12), it's time to head to your growing space and use the "observe and interact" technique (see pp34–37). Try to come up with a clear vision of how you could implement the idea and then create a detailed to-do list.

A runner-bean archway utilizing the area above a path between raised beds takes up far less space in the ground than two wigwams – I got this idea from a post online.

THE INTERNET CAN
BE A BRILLIANT
"IDEAS GENERATOR"
AND A SOURCE
OF SMALL-SPACE
OPPORTUNITIES
AND SOLUTIONS
FOR YOUR GARDEN.

SMALL-SPACE SOLUTIONS

I try to apply as many different space-optimizing ideas as possible in my raised beds to grow the most food I can.

In a limited growing space, I've found the following six methods make the biggest difference.

A. Grow crops in pots

Growing bulky plants in pots has significantly extended my usable growing area. Potatoes can quickly fill beds so I've started growing them in large containers. Grown in pots rather than in the ground, potatoes are highly productive and, more importantly, movable! Recently filled compost bins also make excellent temporary "containers" for pumpkins and courgettes – simply add a large handful of compost when transplanting seedlings into them.

B. Plug gaps

Despite careful planning, gaps will inevitably appear in the garden, and in containers and planters too. Fortunately, I tend to grow more seedlings than I need as an insurance policy so I always have plants to fill spaces. Dwarf French beans, owing to their compact nature, make fantastic gap pluggers, along with edible flowers and annual herbs.

C. Utilize edges

Raised beds with sides offer a solid surface that can be used as a base for a vertical trellis.

This makes a great space-saving alternative to an A-frame or wigwam for growing peas or climbing beans, and frees up bed space for other crops.

D. Store water
Crops need plenty of water, but in small gardens there may only be enough space for a single water butt. A great solution is to store water in clean 5–10 litre (1-2 gallon) containers. Fill these up with rainwater and place in a shady corner, between pots, or wherever you can fit them in.

E. Plant in corners
There is often a small space in the corner of raised beds or containers that is perfect for a trailing nasturtium with edible flowers and leaves or strawberries. Tumbling tomatoes and some squash varieties also work well and although they take up some path space, I'm happy to trade that for an increase in harvests.

F. Split up beds
A surprisingly effective way of organizing and planting up small spaces is to split an empty area into sections – a method popularly known as "square-foot gardening". Use lengths of string to mark out each planting block and help you visualize the finished plan. If you enjoy planning, you might want to take a photo on your phone and use a photo-editing app to note down which crop will go in each block.

TIP

REPURPOSE CLEAN, EMPTY, 2-LITRE (3½-PINT) SCREW-TOP BOTTLES TO STORE WATER AND USE AS HANDY WATERING CANS.

TRIALS AND EXPERIMENTS

MAKE CHANGES TO OPTIMIZE YOUR GARDEN

Experimentation is not only enjoyable but also makes a positive impact on the productivity and efficiency of your garden over the long term. I'll explain how to use trials to increase your knowledge and skills.

MICROCLIMATES CAN MAKE A BIG DIFFERENCE SO IT'S IMPORTANT TO CREATE A BESPOKE LIST OF GO-TO VARIETIES THAT GROW WELL IN YOUR PARTICULAR LOCATION.

CHOOSING VARIETIES

Trialling different varieties of the same crop is a great way to start experimenting. We all have a favourite or stand-by – my default beetroot variety, for example, is 'Boltardy', which gives me consistent results year on year. Sticking with it, however, risks missing out on a more productive staple variety or one that may offer a different flavour.

Every gardener should consider having two separate lists for reference when making a planting plan or putting in a seed order. The first consists of your staples: a "hero" variety for each crop that is tasty, easy to grow, consistent, and abundant. On the second, "specials" list are more unusual varieties that will add magic to your garden as well as excitement to your cooking. Try adding up to five specials for each crop that meets the following criteria:

- Great for small spaces
- Different-coloured flowers
- Different-coloured produce
- Pest or disease resistant
- Heritage variety
- Unusual-shaped root, fruit, or leaves
- Exceptional taste

COMPARING PERFORMANCE

Once you've settled on your "hero" crop, create a shortlist of three (maximum seven) other varieties of the same crop that have the most potential to be a new staple or a "special". Now you're ready to start the trial.

Sowing

Treat the seeds for each variety in exactly the same way using the same timing, location, method, and compost to ensure a fair test. If you're growing in modules, for example, transplant the different seedlings into the same raised bed. Also, grow a minimum of six to seven plants for comparison purposes because the differences between just one single plant of variety A versus variety B can be substantial. For large vegetable plants, such as courgettes and kale, reduce this minimum number to three.

Harvesting

Make notes of your findings (including weather conditions) and then try the same trial with a different crop. Focus on two to three different crops every growing season and you'll soon have a well-rounded list of great varieties. But don't view this list as final: it is a work in progress and every small change will help to increase productivity.

After much trialling, I've settled on three different beetroot – 'Chioggia' (*left*), 'Boltardy' (*middle*), and 'Burpees Golden' (*right*).

TIP

WHY NOT TRY AN
ALTERNATIVE CROP?
I'M CURRENTLY
COMPARING YIELDS
OF BROAD BEANS
WITH FIELD BEANS
AFTER OTHER
GROWERS – WHO
CONDUCTED THE
SAME TRIAL –
REPORTED GREAT
SUCCESS WITH
FIELD BEANS.

COMPARING GROWING METHODS

I also enjoy trialling different methods of growing the same crop because you need only one variety for the experiment. You could compare results from direct sowing versus module sowing, or experiment with different sowing, transplanting, and thinning distances.

Direct or module?

Last year I was forced to grow swede in modules owing to major vole damage to plants sown direct. Surprisingly, the yields of module-sown swede were similar to those sown direct. Despite this result, I find direct sowing easier and remain convinced that direct-sown seedlings make healthier plants because their roots are not disturbed by transplanting. Choose the method that gives you the best results or the one you enjoy the most.

Be flexible with distances

Many of the recommended spacings on the back of seed packets can be taken with a pinch of salt and you can often grow crops closer together for bigger yields. Also, some varieties are smaller or more upright than others, so you can reduce the space between them. Experiment with the varieties you grow and note when you reach optimal production. Broad beans, potatoes, salads, garlic, onions, and leeks are all suitable and I suggest you start by comparing three distances using the following formula:

- **Distance 1** Recommended distance
- **Distance 2** 20 per cent closer than the recommended distance
- **Distance 3** 50 per cent closer than the recommended distance

When it comes to harvesting a crop, for example onions, choose either a whole row or an equal-size block for all distances and compare the yield in terms of weight and size of bulb. Jot down the findings in your notebook so you can refer to them at the start of future growing seasons.

GROW SOMETHING NEW

My favourite annual experiment is to try out two or three edible crops I've never grown before. I don't expect too much, yet have often been amazed by the performance of crops, particularly oca, daikon radish, and spaghetti squash. The excitement of harvesting something totally new is akin to picking the first peas or strawberries of the season and I urge you to try it!

EMBRACE NEW IDEAS

Over the years, watching videos of gardeners in other climates has had a tremendous influence on the way I garden. There are so many incredible ideas, processes, and methods out there, such as Korean Natural Farming (KNF) (see p139). Along with no-dig principles, KNF has now become an integral part of how I grow food.

EXPERIMENTS ARE GREAT TOOLS FOR IMPROVING YOUR SKILLSET AND KEEPING YOU ENGAGED, AS WELL AS A MEANS OF EXPRESSING YOUR GARDENING STYLE.

Amaranth (*opposite*), which I recently trialled, has been a real success. Oca (*above*), the first unusual vegetable I grew, soon became a staple but although Aztec broccoli (*left*) grew well the flavour wasn't standout.

NATURAL FEEDS

MAKE YOUR OWN CHEMICAL-FREE CONCENTRATES

The calcium in eggshells (which is easy to extract) and both comfrey and nettles can be processed to make concentrated liquid feeds. I'll show you how to use these natural ingredients to boost plant health.

EGGSHELL EXTRACT

Put eggshells to good use by following this recipe to produce a concentrated liquid that is is extremely high in calcium.

Plants require continuous supplies of calcium, and eggshells are a wonderful source of this mineral. Rather than putting them on the compost heap, you can make eggshells into a concentrated feed. This recipe for eggshell extract is adapted from the vinegar-extraction process in Nigel Palmer's book, *The Regenerative Grower's Guide to Garden Amendments*.

Equipment and ingredients
- Shells from around 20 eggs, preferably organic
- Baking tray
- Two 0.3–0.5 litre (½–1 pint) jars with lids
- Wooden spoon or spatula
- Raw/unpasteurized apple cider vinegar (around 500ml/1pt)
- Bowl

1. Lay out the eggshells on a baking tray and put in a hot oven (200°C/Gas Mark 6) for 20 minutes. This makes them brittle and easier for nutrient extraction.
2. Place the eggshells into the jar and roughly crush them into smaller pieces using the spoon or spatula. They should fill the bottom fifth of the jar.
3. Pour the apple cider vinegar into the jar leaving a space of 2.5cm (1in) at the top. The mixture may froth so put the lid on loosely and place the jar in the bowl to catch any overspill. Leave the bowl and jar somewhere out of direct sunlight, with good airflow, and at a constant temperature (I leave mine on top of the fridge) for two weeks.
4. Decant the liquid into the other jar using a sieve, put the lid on tightly, and label. This liquid has a high concentration of calcium so you will need approximately 5–10ml (1–2 teaspoons) for a full, 10-litre (2-gallon) watering can. Water the soil around your plants (not the leaves) with the concentrate about twice a month and give a weekly application to fruiting plants like tomatoes that are under cover.

This mixture will keep for a year in a cool dark place. You can repeat the process once more by adding vinegar to the leftover eggshells and leaving for two weeks. Then place the shells on the compost heap.

TIP

STORE WASHED EGGSHELLS IN A JAR UNTIL YOU HAVE ENOUGH. IF YOU DON'T EAT EGGS, ASK FRIENDS OR NEIGHBOURS TO SAVE SHELLS.

"VINEGAR EXTRACTS CALCIUM FROM THE EGGSHELLS TO MAKE A WATER-SOLUBLE FEED PERFECT FOR PLANTS.

FEEDS FROM FOLIAGE

Using either nettles or comfrey, try this simple low-odour recipe to feed your plants.

TIP

'BOCKING 14' IS THE BEST COMFREY VARIETY TO GROW. IT DOESN'T SELF-SEED AND PRODUCES ABUNDANT FOLIAGE.

Nettles are rich in nitrogen and comfrey is rich in potassium. Seedlings and leafy greens require nitrogen while potassium is essential for good fruit production, which makes it the perfect feed for vegetables such as tomatoes and squash. The usual method when making liquid feeds is to leave the foliage in water for two weeks to decompose. While this works well, it smells terrible and can linger on skin and clothing so I prefer to use this nose-friendly version. Simply add the diluted feed to your watering can.

Equipment and ingredients
- Large bucket/container with at least 20 litres (4½ gallons) capacity
- Nettle or comfrey foliage
- Gloves
- A flat piece of wood that fits inside the container
- Heavy stones or bricks
- Shears

Note: The size of container will depend on the volume of nettles or comfrey you can source. It will also need a fairly heavy lid, such as an old paving slab, to keep off the rain but allow for some airflow.

1. Wearing gloves, use shears to collect your plant material. The best time is early in the morning when plants have a higher moisture content. Collect roughly twice as much as will fit into your container.

2. Once the container is full, roughly chop up the stems and leaves with the shears. The volume of material should reduce by half. Top up with more material and chop this up too.

3. Put the container in a sheltered spot, place the wood on top of the chopped material and weigh it down with the stones or bricks. The wood will help disperse the weight of the bricks more evenly. Loosely place the lid on top and leave for 3–10 weeks.

4. After 3 weeks, you can pour off the light brown liquid and use it diluted: 1 part to 20 parts water. For a more concentrated result leave the container for a further 5–10 weeks. Almost all the stems and leaves will have decomposed and the resulting very dark brown liquid can be used in a dilution of 1:100. This equates to 100ml in a 10-litre watering can (or 3½ fl oz in a 2-gallon can). The feed can be bottled and will keep for a year in a dark, cool shed or garage. Leftover plant material can be composted.

FOLIAR FEEDS

Plants can absorb nutrients from foliar feeding in a matter of minutes and this is the best and most direct method for dealing with plant mineral deficiencies. Here are some tips on how and when to feed:

- Feed once a week maximum and be consistent. I opt for once every two weeks.
- For best results, apply foliar feeds on cooler days.
- Feeds work more efficiently when humidity is high.
- Ideally, apply early on an overcast day, when the dew hasn't evaporated.

There are a range of tools you can use to apply foliar feeds. For small spaces use a hand spray but for larger growing areas I recommend a 5-litre (1-gallon) pump-action pressure sprayer.

TIP

FOR HEALTHY PLANTS, APPLY FOLIAR FEEDS AS WELL AS WATERING WITH DILUTED FEEDS ON A CONSISTENT BASIS.

Spraying kale with diluted nettle feed is the quickest way to give the plants an extra boost of nutrients and promote healthy growth.

HERBS
AND FLOWERS

Diversify the mix of plants to create a thriving vegetable garden

THE MISSING ELEMENTS

FOR A BEAUTIFUL AND PRODUCTIVE PLOT

Aromatic herbs produce huge amounts of flavour for the small amount of space they occupy. Combine them with flowers and you'll attract bees, butterflies, and other pollinators. I'll explain how to integrate both into your vegetable plot.

PLANTING GREATER NUMBERS OF HERBS AND FLOWERS AMONG THE VEGETABLES I GROW BENEFITS THE WHOLE GARDEN.

For me, adding herbs and flowers was the missing element that tied everything in the garden together. Flowers such as calendula pack a punch with a splash of orange that lifts a corner of the garden, while a single coriander plant will flavour countless meals and salads. By integrating herbs and flowers with your vegetable crops, you significantly increase diversity, and create a healthy, productive, and sustainable plot.

ISLAND BLOCKS

Finding a way of growing herbs and flowers in my vegetable plot while trying to produce as much food as possible over the season was a big challenge. However, I've come up with a simple method of growing them alongside my staple and secondary vegetable crops that doesn't impact or confuse the planting plan. I like to split a bed up into sections or blocks that run the length of a raised bed and found the best way to combine annual herbs and flowers was to create a dedicated "end block" in some of them. Each of these herb and flower blocks has three key elements, which I've outlined below.

Vertical structure

This serves two purposes. The first is to grow either an edible climber or an ornamental annual, such as runner beans or sweet peas, which uses the space efficiently and adds structure to the garden. The second is to create shade. Herbs such as parsley, basil, and coriander will do well on the shady side of a wigwam for example, or plant some extra leafy greens, such as spinach.

Annual Herbs

Growing a few different annual herbs per block gives me plenty to share with neighbours and friends. I don't plant these herbs closely together, which ensures there is enough space for flowers around or in-between them. Also, try allowing some herbs to flower so they attract pollinators. Then, save and dry the seeds either for cooking or sowing again next year. Coriander is one herb that ticks all the boxes.

Dual-purpose flowers

With the exception of a small handful of flowers, I always grow those with edible petals, such as calendula and nasturtiums. Planted throughout the garden, they offer vibrant bursts of colour in a predominantly green space as well as adding interest and flavour to the food I cook. The flowers also attract beneficial insects that not only pollinate crops but also act as natural pest controllers.

GARDEN ESSENTIALS

In summary, incorporating herbs and edible flowers is a fantastic way to increase the beauty and productivity of any vegetable garden. They have become indispensable to my garden and made it a more interesting, diverse, and enjoyable space to work and relax in. In the following pages, I'll discuss the key herbs and flowers, explain how to grow them, and list all the benefits of these fantastic plants.

In this island block you can see borage and calendula interplanted with parsley, dill, and coriander. The latter two are in full flower.

ANNUAL HERBS

MUST-GROW PLANTS WITH FANTASTIC FLAVOUR

Annual herbs are the unsung heroes of any kitchen garden. They can be grown in a small area and need little maintenance yet are arguably the most useful and versatile of all edible plants when it comes to cooking.

TIP

CRUSH 20 GREEN CORIANDER SEEDS WITH A GARLIC CLOVE, THEN COMBINE WITH 50G (1¾OZ) OF SOFT BUTTER. IT'S DELICIOUS ON COOKED VEGGIES.

Aromatic green herbs are easy to grow and the freshly picked leaves are far superior in taste to the dried versions. You can utilize succession planting (see p152) to ensure continuous cropping. Some annual herbs, such as parsley, may retain leaves for picking in mild winters while others can be preserved for a taste of summer in colder months. Annual herbs take up very little space so why not grow more than you'll need and share harvests? I've chosen four must-grow leafy herbs that I would never be without.

A. Basil

You can start off basil from late winter by sowing 8–10 seeds per 5cm (2in) or 7cm (2¾in) pot at a depth of 1cm (½in) and placing it on a sunny windowsill. When seedlings are big enough to handle, pot on individually into 7cm (2¾in) pots to grow on, and then 4–6 weeks later transplant into their final growing position. Wait until all risk of frost has passed before planting basil outside or grow it on under cover. Basil loves warmth but prefers to be out of direct sunlight, so a semi-shady position is ideal. Pinch out the growing tips regularly to promote strong, bushy growth and keep sowing until summer.

B. Coriander

As with basil, I like to start my coriander under cover – two weeks before your last frost date at the earliest. Sow 6–7 seeds in each 7cm (2¾in) pot, cover with a fine layer of compost and thin to 4–5 plants per pot. Once seedlings are 7cm (2¾in) tall, plant out the clumps of seedlings in their final position and sow a new batch so you don't run out: coriander can quickly run to seed in hot weather. Additional sowings can be made up until mid-summer.

Alternatively, once the risk of frost has passed, sow seed direct in drills that are 1cm (½in) deep and spaced 10cm (4in) apart. Thin to leave 8–10cm (3–4in) between plants. Coriander leaves don't freeze well but I add fresh green or dried seeds to many dishes.

C. Dill

Seeds of this feathery-leaved herb can be sown direct in a sunny spot around your last frost date. Sow thinly into 1cm (½in) deep trenches spaced 15cm (6in) apart. Thin seedlings to one every 15cm (6in) and keep plants well watered. I recommend supporting the tall stems with sticks or wire mesh to prevent plants blowing over in the wind. You can continue sowing until early summer.

D. Parsley (flat-leaved)

Sow this endlessly useful herb direct, following the timing, depth, thinning and spacing given for dill. Or sow 3–4 seeds per medium-sized module (40-50mm/1½–2in) and thin to 2 seedlings. Grow on and transplant when seedlings are around 7cm (2¾in) tall. Parsley is hardy in mild areas, or you can grow it under cover, harvest right through winter, then enjoy a new flush of its vitamin-rich leaves in early spring before it runs to seed. Parsley grows very well in partial shade.

PERENNIAL HERBS

ESSENTIAL AROMATICS FOR BEDS AND CONTAINERS

To my mind, no garden should be without perennial herbs. They are fantastic for cooking, beautiful to look at, and loved by pollinators. Many are also very easy to raise from cuttings.

TIP

LOOK OUT FOR VARIETIES OF PERENNIAL HERBS WITH UNUSUAL CHARACTERISTICS, SUCH AS DIFFERENCES IN FLAVOUR OR COLOUR.

I find the eight herbs listed below indispensable and would urge you to grow them. They will thrive in a dedicated herb bed or in large pots and containers.

A. Chives

Although chives die back each winter, the flourish of dense new growth that emerges in spring can add so much flavour to so many dishes. You can easily create new plants by dividing clumps into three or four sections in early spring or late autumn. The edible flowers are also beautiful and will attract pollinators. Chives grow well in shadier areas and like slightly damp soil.

B. Lavender

This beautiful plant is worth growing for its fragrance alone, but the flowers will also attract pollinators and you can eat the buds. Lavender grows in similar conditions to rosemary and is best propagated by taking 10cm (4in) cuttings of sideshoots in early summer. Use the plastic-bag method (see lemon verbena) to help with rooting.

C Lemon Verbena

The superior lemon flavour of the leaves makes the best herbal tea ever. Of the eight herbs, this is the most tender. I recommend you insulate the plant during cold snaps or bring it into a greenhouse or cool shed over winter. Propagate by taking 10cm (4in) semi-ripe cuttings, pot them up, cover with a plastic bag to keep them hydrated, and place under cover. Remove the bag after 4–6 weeks.

D. Marjoram

Perhaps one of the most underrated herbs, marjoram can be substituted for oregano (a close relative) in cooking. Use it fresh with tomatoes, in salads, and in pasta dishes. The

best way to propagate marjoram is to divide mature plants into three or four sections in early spring or autumn.

E. Mint

There are so many varieties of mint to choose from, but whichever you grow, a generous handful of fresh leaves steeped in boiling water for a few minutes makes a really refreshing tea. Mint grows well in shade and prefers damper soils but spreads quickly so if you're short of space, grow it in large pots. Mint is easily propagated from 10cm (4in) cuttings taken throughout late spring and summer. Put these in water and then pot up once rooted. Mint dies back each winter.

F. Rosemary

The aromatic leaves can be picked year round, and because rosemary doesn't spread you can grow it confidently in a raised bed. The ideal spot is a warm, sunny position with a free-draining soil. If you live in a wetter region, plant at the end of a raised bed or in containers that are at least 20 litres (4½ gallons) in size.

To increase your stock, take 10cm (4in) cuttings of new growth between mid-spring and early summer and cover with a clear plastic bag (see lemon verbena).

G. Sage

Another kitchen staple, sage grows year round but can lose leaf quality by late winter before a resurgence of growth in spring. Although it works well when dried, I always use fresh leaves. It enjoys similar conditions to rosemary, but can tolerate more moisture in the ground. To propagate, take 15cm (6in) softwood cuttings in mid-spring through to summer.

H. Thyme

This small but mighty herb enjoys full sun and grows well in both raised beds and pots provided they have good drainage. It is evergreen, so you can use it fresh throughout the year, which I prefer, but the leaves also dry well. Take 5–7cm (2–2¾in) cuttings from late spring through summer and use the plastic bag method (see lemon verbena) to promote root growth.

OF ALL THE PERENNIAL HERBS, CHIVES EXCITE ME THE MOST. THE TASTE IS FANTASTIC AND YOUR LOCAL BUMBLEBEE POPULATION WILL LOVE THE FLOWERS.

MULTI-PURPOSE FLOWERS

COLOURFUL AND EDIBLE BLOOMS FOR US AND POLLINATORS

I like to grow plants that serve more than one purpose and all those described here are beautiful, as well as being pollinator magnets. Many also happen to be edible.

POTAGER-INSPIRED GARDENING IS A FANTASTIC WAY TO HELP CREATE A BIODIVERSITY BALANCE IN YOUR GARDEN.

VEGETABLE FLOWERS

I always enjoy experimenting with my vegetable crops and recently I've allowed a few to continue growing just to see what happens. My experiment has proved to be a lazy yet effective way of growing an abundance of flowers to add colour to the garden, as well as attracting pollinators. Many are also edible, providing a tasty crop of either flowers, pods, or seeds. Below are some of my favourites.

A. Coriander

The tiny white flowers soon turn into round green seeds that you can eat fresh or dried and use whole or crushed.

B. Courgettes

Choose male flowers for picking and eating, always leaving some on the plant so fruit-producing female flowers are pollinated.

C. Fennel

Amazing heads of edible flowers are followed by aromatic seeds, which can be used in savoury dishes and spice mixes.

D. Kale

Leave overwintered kale plants to send up edible flower shoots in spring – a delicious alternative to purple sprouting broccoli. Let the flower shoots develop fully for pollinators.

E. Leeks

The beautiful chive-like flowers erupt at the top of tall stems and are loved by bees.

F. Lettuce

The small dandelion-like flowers of bolted lettuce bring a fantastic burst of yellow to the garden. Try leaving the odd lettuce plant in the corner of a bed to bloom and see for yourself how lovely they look.

G. Pak choi

The flower stems and the flowers themselves are edible and give off a beautiful fragrance when grown over winter in a greenhouse and allowed to flower in early spring.

H. Radish

The stems produce a huge display of edible white flowers. Leave some to develop into young green seed pods, which add a refreshing crunch to salads.

POLLINATOR-FRIENDLY PLANTS

For me, a combination of different types of plants, as seen in traditional French potager-style plots, is vital for attracting a range of beneficial insects to pollinate your crops and help reduce any potential pest problems. All the flowers listed are easy to grow, their blooms add bursts of colour, and many taste delicious in summer salads.

EDIBLE ANNUALS

As well as allowing some vegetables to flower and set seed, I also like to squeeze in colourful edible flowers for added pleasure at mealtimes. Here are the five annual edible flowers I grow most often.

A. Borage

Bristly-leaved borage produces little blue flowers that taste amazing. They are my absolute favourite for decorating side-dishes and desserts. Sow under cover and plant out seedlings after all risk of frost has passed.

B. Calendula

The pot marigold has been a firm favourite in kitchen gardens since medieval times. Start off in modules then transplant to a sunny position where it produces masses of bright-orange blooms. The petals are perfect for use in salads, cool summer drinks, and rice dishes. Sow seeds in early spring for flowers through summer and into autumn.

C. Cornflower

This traditional cottage-garden flower will add a stunning, vibrant blue to your growing area. 'Blue boy' is a fantastic edible cornflower that can be sown direct or started off in pots during spring for flowers throughout summer. Other shades such as pink and lilac are also available.

D. Nasturtium

You can eat the leaves, flowers, and even the young seed pods of this versatile plant. Nasturtiums are so easy to grow that once established they can start popping up everywhere. Either sow direct once all risk of frost has passed, or start in modules under cover around the last frost date and transplant. Nasturtiums add bright, warm colour and there are several varieties.

E. Viola

Pretty, multi-coloured violas are very easy to grow and widely available as plug plants. Always choose those with edible flowers – *Viola tricolour*, *Viola cornuta*, and *Viola odorata*. Their small stature makes them perfect for the edges of raised beds, and the flowers look fantastic in salads. Pick regularly to extend the flowering period.

TIP

IF, LIKE ME, YOU ARE PASSIONATE ABOUT POLLINATORS, I RECOMMEND SEEKING OUT BOOKS ON BEE-FRIENDLY PLANTS AND GARDENING.

NETTLES

THE MOST USEFUL WEED

Many weeds get a bad press, but every weed is part of an ecosystem, and for me, nettles are the most beneficial weed of them all. I'd like to explain why it's a good idea to grow more nettles in and around your garden.

The common nettle is one of the easiest wild plants to identify and has been used by traditional herbalists for centuries. Most people view it as just a weed with an irritating sting, but this remarkable plant deserves more appreciation.

PEST CONTROL

Nettles in sheltered areas make fantastic aphid magnets – I am always surprised by just how many aphids gather on the stems and leaves. We can turn this to our advantage by using nettles to lure aphids away from precious food crops. A lovely comment I received on one of my YouTube videos sums this idea up nicely: "Pests are just hungry creatures, so give them something to eat". Letting extra nettles grow for the aphids does just that.

BENEFICIAL INSECTS

Nettles are the food source for ladybird larvae, which consume vast quantities of aphids as they grow. They are also the preferred food of many caterpillars, including the red admiral, comma, tortoiseshell, and – my favourite butterfly – the peacock. If you have space, always aim to have a wild patch of nettles in a sheltered spot for these beautiful garden pollinators.

NUTRIENT-RICH

Nettles are often classed as a superfood. The young tender leaves and growing tips can be used in many dishes and contain large amounts of vitamins A and K, as well as some of the B vitamins. They are also high in calcium, magnesium, and iron, while 100g (3½oz) of blanched nettle leaves provide 20 per cent of your dietary fibre needs. The great thing about nettles is that the nutrients don't leach out when cooked. Even the seeds are edible and packed with goodness, plus essential fatty acids. A teaspoon of nettle seeds thrown into a smoothie is a great way to consume them. Just remember to pick them wearing gloves!

SOIL AND PLANT HEALTH

I like to use nettles as a mulch for fruit trees, when adopting the "chop, move, and drop" method (see p66), and the green material makes a high-quality activator to speed up the composting process. Add only the stems and leaves to the compost bin and try to avoid adding seeds. Another brilliant way to use nettles is as an ingredient in organic feed (see p180).

TIP

MID JULY TO EARLY AUGUST IS THE BEST TIME TO GO CATERPILLAR SPOTTING IN A PATCH OF NETTLES. JUST DON'T WEAR SHORTS!

Allow nettles to grow in and around your garden to attract beneficial insects. The chopped leaves make a nutritious mulch (*top*) and the plant is a food source for butterfly larvae. Inside this nettle leaf (*above*) I found a red admiral caterpillar feeding.

UNDER COVER NETTLES

There has always been a patch of volunteer nettles at one end of the solar tunnel. Last year, I decided to leave them because I was growing tomatoes in there. Aphids were all over the nettles yet there were none on the tomatoes. Watching a dozen or so ladybird larvae get to work on the aphids was even more exciting.

SUPPORTIVE FLOWERS

HOW TO BRIGHTEN UP YOUR GARDEN

Although I strive to grow as many edibles as possible, I always make space for a handful of beautiful flowers. Sow seed in spring, and both you and your garden insects will reap the benefits.

Many of us have a favourite flower, or one that reminds us of a special person or place, so by all means incorporate a cherished flower into your plot. In addition to the edible flowers listed earlier (see pp192–195), the following are well worth growing and all are easy to raise from seed (you probably already have dandelions!).

A. Cosmos
I was inspired to grow cosmos after a visit to Liz Zorab's garden at Byther Farm in Monmouthshire, where I was taken aback by the beauty and structure these flowers added to the borders. Colours vary from white through to pink, deep red, and yellow, and there are also dwarf varieties available for smaller spaces. They couldn't be easier to grow and have quickly become a must-have flower in the garden.

Cosmos seed can be sown direct where it is to flower after the risk of frost has passed. Alternatively, sow a couple of seeds per small module on the surface of the compost and cover very lightly. Thin to the strongest seedling and transplant into their final

> " "
>
> DANDELIONS SHOULD BE LEFT TO FLOWER IN EARLY SPRING – THEIR FLOWERS ARE A MUCH-NEEDED SOURCE OF POLLEN AND NECTAR FOR BEES.

position when their first true leaves appear. Space plants 20–25cm (8–10in) apart, then leave them to it. Tall varieties may need staking if they are in an exposed area.

B. Dandelions
Although considered a weed, dandelions are an essential food source for pollinators in early spring when few other flowers are in bloom. While I certainly don't want them in my raised beds, I let them grow and flower naturally on the path and around the garden. Dandelion leaves are bitter yet edible and the flowers can be used to make wine or a syrupy alternative to honey. I prefer to leave the plants for the bees to make some real honey!

C. Foxgloves
This might seem like an unusual suggestion, but the common deep-pink foxglove is a beautiful flower that is especially loved by bumblebees. Those with larger gardens or allotments will often come across self-sown foxgloves, which can be lifted and grown on in containers or at the edge of a raised bed. They make an easy and colourful addition to the garden. To grow foxgloves from

scratch, buy seeds of *Digitalis purpurea* and check it is the true wild form. Foxgloves are biennials, growing leaves in their first year after sowing but not producing flowers until the second year.

D. Sweet Peas
These were the first non-edible flowers I grew from seed, as I wanted to enjoy them without having to buy bunches from the greengrocer's. I love their perfume when I'm doing some gardening in the evening and they add a splash of vertical colour in the garden. Sweet peas are generous: keep picking and more flowers will follow.

Although the choice of sweet pea varieties available to gardeners is huge, I always buy a scented mix of different colours. To my eye, the random effect from a mixed packet works much better than combining individual varieties. As with garden peas, I sow sweet peas in modules but earlier – eight weeks before the last frost date – then transplant them around four weeks later.

TIP

SWEET PEAS ARE SUPER-EASY TO SAVE SEED FROM. SIMPLY LEAVE THE PODS ON THE PLANTS TO DRY, COLLECT THE PEAS, AND STORE IN A JAR.

COMMUNITY
GARDENING

Connect with other growers, sharing skills and harvests

CO-SUFFICIENCY

CONTRIBUTING TO YOUR COMMUNITY

Given our busy lives, it isn't practical or feasible for most of us to be self-sufficient in homegrown food – but co-sufficiency can help to make ourselves and our communities strong, productive, and resilient.

THE FUTURE OF EVERY COMMUNITY LIES IN CAPTURING THE PASSION, IMAGINATION, AND RESOURCES OF ITS PEOPLE.
DR ERNESTO SIROLLI, (1950–) ECONOMIST

There isn't a single definition of co-sufficiency (an abbreviation of community sufficiency), but to my mind it involves combining a degree of individual self-sufficiency with shared initiatives to bring multiple benefits to a community. This chapter will explore some of the many ways in which we can work with other like-minded people to open up opportunities and enjoy positive experiences, from creating a gardening club to the satisfaction of giving.

TEAMWORK

I believe our own personal projects are vital in that they give us valuable time to ourselves, but that working with others who share our passions and interests is also beneficial. One of the best things about collaborating with other gardeners is that it gives us the opportunity to get a lot done in a short space of time. This can be a real blessing, especially if we have a big project, such as fencing one of the garden boundaries, that needs additional input or extra pairs of hands. Working as a team can also increase motivation hugely, as well as being great fun!

SHARING PRODUCE

Teaming up with others who have a similar aim can help realize your ambitions. For example, if your common goal is reducing your food bill, perhaps each gardener could focus on growing bulk quantities of a couple of staple crops each season, then at harvest time everyone shares the produce. It's

much easier and more efficient than trying to grow as much as you can of too many different things.

Food is one of the few things that connect all of us no matter what our background or culture, and growing food together is a fantastic basis for creating a co-sufficient community. From sharing seeds and harvests to lending a tool or a helping hand when needed, we can achieve so much more when we get others involved.

I'm always blown away by how much can be achieved when a small group of passionate gardeners come together.

COMMUNITY GROWING PROJECTS

CREATING SHARED RESOURCES

When we get together, either as individuals or as an established group, a few enthusiastic and energetic gardeners can create fantastic community projects. I'd recommend starting with a community compost scheme or seed bank.

TIP

ONE OF THE BEST WAYS TO HELP YOUR COMMUNITY IS TO SHARE YOUR SURPLUS, BE IT INFORMATION, FOOD, OR PLANTS!

COMMUNITY COMPOST

Schemes are often run by a group of growers, with each participant contributing raw materials to be composted in exchange for a share of finished compost. It offers gardeners in villages, small towns, and suburban areas the opportunity to pool materials together to create a respectable volume of compost. The composting process is more efficient when done on a large scale – bigger heaps heat up faster – and members get good-quality compost fairly quickly.

If you have limited space for composting bins but want to get hold of high-quality compost, a community composting scheme is a great solution. There are many different ways of establishing your own scheme, but here are some pointers:

• Keep the scheme small and informal, perhaps based on four to six members. The person who donates space in their garden for the composting area should be rewarded appropriately – perhaps with a larger share of compost. The site should be easily accessible to all members.

• If you need to source additional materials, refer to the list of suggestions on page 52. Cardboard from local shops and vegetable scraps from cafés and restaurants are especially useful.

• Share the costs and workload between all members, and always divide finished compost fairly. A good way of measuring out compost by volume is to use 20-litre (4-gallon) buckets.

• Use hot-composting methods whenever possible (see p62) for faster turnaround and higher yields.

COMMUNITY SEED BANK

Working as a group, members of a community seed bank or library save, store, and share seed varieties with local gardeners. The focus is usually on heritage varieties that are exempt from copyright legislation. Plants registered under Plant Breeders Rights (PBR) legislation are protected by copyright and can't be sold or reproduced, usually for a period of around 25 years.

One fantastic example of this is Lampeter Seed Library in Wales. Set up by a group of like-minded gardeners and permaculturists, people can visit their regular stall at the local farmers' market to donate seeds, swap seeds, and find out which varieties grow well in the local climate. The library also runs regular courses where you can learn how to save your own seeds.

A community seed bank increases a community's co-sufficiency because there is less need to source seeds externally and members have access to the highest quality seed stock from varieties suited to their local climate. The cost of seeds is also greatly reduced, which saves members money.

For more help on community growing projects and useful links check out the Resources section (p216).

Solid and well-built, this setup is ideal for a community compost project (*left*).

Seed banks and libraries are great places to find unusual varieties of crops (*right*).

CONNECTED GARDENING

LINK UP WITH OTHER GROWERS

Staying connected, either by working with others or utilizing online resources, helps me achieve more in my growing space while enjoying the benefits of socializing and learning about the hobby I love.

Whether it be working with like-minded people on a garden project, discussing recent trials and experiments together one summer's evening, or increasing your knowledge via a podcast, what I call "connected gardening" – the interactions in person or via technology – brings so many benefits. My favourite times in the garden have always been those spent gardening with my dad or with another gardener, and when that isn't possible, listening to podcasts is a great alternative. Take a look at some of the ways you can interact with other gardeners, seek out new ideas, and have fun.

GARDENING PARTNER

A great way to get big gardening projects completed and increase productivity is to connect with another gardener. Gardening with a partner is not only enjoyable, it will also help you grow more food.

You could start by asking friends who you know would appreciate some help in the garden. The two of you can keep each other motivated during challenging periods, enjoy sharing successes (and plants), and help each other with big gardening jobs.

I'd recommend setting aside a morning or an afternoon per month to visit each other's gardens and that you plan in advance which jobs you'll share. That might be building new raised beds, weeding, or harvesting potatoes. These sessions are an excellent opportunity to chat, ask questions, and come up with solutions to recent gardening problems.

" "

GARDENING FRIENDS MAKE IDEAL PARTNERS BECAUSE THEY UNDERSTAND THE INEVITABLE UPS AND DOWNS OF GROWING FOOD.

SKILL SHARING

We all have valuable skills and knowledge that we can contribute and share. For example, you might be a compost wizard and keen to teach others how to make high-quality compost; or you might be brilliant at saving seeds of varieties that grow well in your local climate and can offer them to gardeners nearby. Skill-sharing is a great way to connect with people and you both learn something new in the process.

Sharing big gardening tasks makes life much easier. My dad is kindly helping me to change the layout of the raised beds to increase growing space.

GARDENING WITH A PARTNER IS ALSO AN EXCUSE TO INDULGE IN PLENTY OF TEA AND CAKE!

GARDENING GROUP

Why not join or set up a gardening group? When between four and seven passionate individuals get together, they form a gardening "mastermind" – a forum where members can discuss ideas, find solutions, offer advice, and celebrate successes. Having a close-knit community of gardeners strengthens bonds between members and you may even create a loyal and lasting group of good friends. Here are some suggestions for projects and activities once your group is up and running:

• **Work parties** Many hands make light work, and a gardening work party can achieve a serious amount in a surprisingly short time. It's a great way to blitz your garden, getting the whole area spring cleaned or winter-prepped in a morning.

• **Supper clubs** You could have a monthly supper club, inspired by produce from your gardens. It's a great opportunity to eat homegrown food, share thoughts and ideas, and ask for help with particular issues.

• **Film nights** My local permaculture group holds regular film nights showing videos, short films, and movies on sustainability topics or featuring amazing growing projects.

• **Visits and courses** Most gardening groups really enjoy looking around other gardens or visiting new gardening projects. Also, why not try an interesting day or weekend course where you learn something new together, from beekeeping to making an outdoor pizza oven?

• **Book club** I'm particularly interested in adapting growing methods from other climates for my own garden and often find great ideas in books. Why not set up a gardening book club, choose a new book, then meet every couple of months to discuss it?

GET ONLINE

While it might not always be possible to meet up with gardening friends in person, try visiting local online gardening groups or forums. Online platforms are great virtual spaces to meet other people with similar interests, share ideas, and ask for advice. Podcasts are also brilliant resources to further your gardening knowledge, and I find working in the garden is an ideal opportunity to listen to a podcast. For a list of my suggestions see the Resources section at the back of the book (see p216).

What you listen to doesn't always have to be garden-related either. Audiobooks are a great alternative to podcasts and my dad, for example, regularly listens to them while doing routine jobs around the smallholding. Whatever your preference, you'll not only spend time in the garden listening to something you enjoy or find interesting, but you may also notice an increase in your productivity. Five minutes of weeding can quickly turn into half an hour – a blessing if there's a lot of weeding to do!

WHEN CARRYING OUT STRAIGHTFORWARD TASKS, I FIND TIME FLIES IF I LISTEN TO A PODCAST AND I GET SO MUCH MORE DONE!

It's important to view your garden as a space for relaxation and enjoyment as well as a productive working area.

THE GIFT OF GIVING

ACTS OF KINDNESS

All of us who enjoy the benefits of a garden can help and inspire others to start their growing journey. Just as small changes in the garden can have a big impact, small actions can also make a big difference in our communities.

A garden of your own is an amazing asset that you can use to teach, encourage, and help others to grow their own food. Amelia Earheart, writer and aviator (1897–1939) once wrote, "A single act of kindness throws out roots in all directions, and the roots spring up and make new trees." I feel there are three key areas where, as gardeners, we can take small steps to make the biggest differences.

SEEDS AND SEEDLING SHARING

Often all it takes for someone to fall in love with gardening is to be given a few seeds or seedlings and experience the rewards of growing and eating their own freshly harvested produce. You could, for example, display edible plants in pots outside your home with a "help yourself" sign to encourage people to have a go. Salads, peas, and annual herbs are all perfect as they are simple to grow and offer quick returns.

Seeds, too, are a wonderful resource to share with local primary schools for growing projects, or you could take them along to a community seed swap run by a local gardening group. You'll meet like-minded people and pick up new or different varieties of seed to try in return.

ENCOURAGING WILDLIFE

Nature is a resource shared by everyone in the community and gardeners have a whole range of options for encouraging our precious wildlife for the benefit of all. Install bug hotels, bird boxes, a bird feeder, a bird bath, a bat box, a solitary bee tower, or just leave a patch of lawn to grow wild. These are just a few ways you can make a difference and you'll find more suggestions in the books I recommend for wildlife-friendly gardening in the Resources section (see p216).

SHARING HARVESTS

My third suggestion is to share harvests and excess produce with neighbours and friends in the community. This is a fantastic strategy for getting people interested in growing food because they are won over by how fresh and delicious it tastes. Offering small jam jars of cut flowers or herbs for free is also a great way to give something back and to brighten someone's day.

USUALLY WHEN SOMEONE EXPERIENCES THE TASTE OF THAT FIRST HARVEST, IT IGNITES THEIR PASSION FOR GROWING FOOD.

When selecting produce to be shared with neighbours, I like to add flowers to the display. A splash of colour always draws people's attention.

TIP

IF YOU HAVE A
LARGE GARDEN WHY
NOT CONSIDER
INVITING A GARDEN-
LESS FRIEND TO
ADOPT A BED? IT
WOULD MAKE A
WONDERFUL
BIRTHDAY OR
CHRISTMAS GIFT.

FINAL WORDS

I hope that your biggest takeaway from reading this book is just how much creativity and flexibility there is when it comes to growing your own food. I view gardening as a form of art in that we choose how to design our space, what to grow, and how to grow it based on our own experience. Through trials and experiments, we can explore new ideas and hone techniques, maximizing the potential of our gardens to bring us bountiful harvests and joy.

Out of all the hobbies and pastimes, I firmly believe you'll struggle to find one as diverse as gardening, which can involve practical skills such as making a bench or creating cakes based around homegrown strawberries. You can garden indoors and outdoors – on a windowsill or in a field – pick your favourite tastes and colours, create space for both wildlife and pets, decorate your house with flowers and fill your belly with homegrown harvests. It's no coincidence that health professionals are prescribing gardening as a way of easing depression and anxiety because gardening reconnects us with ourselves and with the natural world.

When a busy growing season is in full swing and we're focused on producing food, it's easy to forget the limitless benefits gardening brings. Now more than ever, it's vital to take time out, sit back, relish your space and feel that huge sense of pride and accomplishment. If you haven't already, I implore you to create a small seating area (even if it's just a camping chair), perhaps get a firepit, and find a corner in your garden where you can enjoy long summer evenings overlooking your kingdom. Every gardener, like every artist, deserves to sit back and admire their creation...

RESOURCES

USEFUL WEBSITES

Seed suppliers
Real Seeds realseeds.co.uk
Tamar Organics tamarorganics.co.uk
Vital Seeds vitalseeds.co.uk

Community growing schemes
Social Farms & Gardens farmgarden.org.uk
The Community Supported Agriculture Network
  https://communitysupportedagriculture.org.uk

Gardening accessories
Seed trays gardentrays.co.uk
Garden snips niwaki.com/garden-snips/
Kneeler niwaki.com/kneeler/
Gardening twine twool.co.uk/shop/classic-twool-twine/
Dry touch gloves goldleaf-gloves.com/drytouch.htm
The Kelly Kettle kellykettle.com

My online courses
Kitchen Garden Fermentation
  kitchengardenfermentation.com
Monthly Planting Plan Course planforabundance.com
  (also see YouTube video: https://www.youtube.com/
  watch?v=nkjeSJQWhZc)

Miscellaneous
Last frost dates plantmaps.com

RECOMMENDED BOOKS

Soil health
Entangled Life, Merlin Sheldrake
Dirt to Soil, Gabe Brown
Kiss the Ground, Josh Tickell
Teaming with Microbes, Jeff Lowenfels
The Living Soil Handbook, Jesse Frost

Grow your own food
Allotment Handbook, DK
A Woman's Garden, Tanya Anderson
Edible Paradise, Vera Greutink
No Dig Organic Home and Garden, Charles Dowding
  and Stephanie Hafferty
No-Till Organic Vegetable Farm, Daniel Mays
The Lean Farm Guide to Growing Vegetables,
  Ben Hartman
*The Regenerative Grower's Guide to Garden
  Amendments*, Nigel Palmer

Wildlife
Gardening for Bumblebees, Dave Goulson
Wildlife Gardening, Kate Bradbury
Wild Your Garden, The Butterfly Brothers

INSPIRATION

YouTubers to follow
Charles Dowding
Edible Acres
Epic Gardening
Happen Films
Liz Zorab – Byther Farm
Simplify Gardening
The Gardening Channel With James Prigioni
The Optimistic Gardener
suburban homestead
Self Sufficient Me

My favourite podcasts
Farmerama Radio
Regenerative Agriculture Podcast
The Anthropocene Reviewed
The No-Till Market Garden Podcast
The Tim Ferriss Show

INDEX

ACKNOWLEDGMENTS

AUTHOR'S ACKNOWLEDGMENTS

First, I want to thank my Publisher Katie and the team at DK for their incredible support – it's such a privilege to work with people who go above and beyond. In particular, I would like to thank Glenda, Lucy, and Ruth who have been there at every single stage of this book's development – thank you for your patience with me during this project! The pages you have created out of the text and photos I sent you have exceeded all my expectations. Thank you, too, to my literary agents, Laura and Olivia, who have been fantastic, allowing me to focus on the creative side of the book process – I really appreciate your publishing expertise!

Writing during a pandemic was a very different experience to my previous two books – escaping to my favourite cafés was no longer an option. Instead, I must thank everyone close to me who, either directly or indirectly, supported the creation of this book. Thanks, in particular, to my dad Steven for making me fall in love with gardening in the first place, and to my mum Clarissa, and sister Fflur, who never fail to put a smile on my face. You have all been so amazing!

To my close friend and fellow gardener Liz: you always have my back and make the time to chat at a minute's notice about literally anything! I'm so excited to see how your new ventures mature and flourish.

A special mention goes to my colleague Sam. Thank you for all your invaluable help and collaboration on @farmer.and.chef, our joint project that inspires gardeners to make tasty meals from their prized harvests. It's been awesome to see you create delicious recipes using produce from my garden.

Finally, I want to thank the wonderful online gardening community for sharing all their successes, tips, failures, lessons, and findings. During the pandemic, this group of growers was like an extended family to me, which grew even bigger as more people took up gardening in 2020. There is so much more that connects us than separates us, and we all have a collective duty to support and nurture every single person who's starting out so we can all make our dream of growing food a reality.

PUBLISHER'S ACKNOWLEDGMENTS

The Publisher would like to thank Christine Keilty for initial design work, Steve Crozier for image retouching and colour work, Francesco Piscitelli for proofreading, and Vanessa Bird for creating the index.

PICTURE CREDITS

The publisher would like to thank the following for their kind permission to reproduce their photographs:

(Key: a-above; b-below/bottom; c-centre; f-far; l-left; r-right; t-top)

Shutterstock.com: meunierd 102ca, Tomasz Klejdysz 135bl, Vidura Dissanayake 193cl; **Dreamstime.com:** Dleonis 114br; **Huw Richards:** 13, 21, 22–23, 28, 29, 31 (a, b, c, d, e, f), 39 (t & br), 45, 48 (t & b), 53 (t, bl, & br), 54, 57, 59, 63 (1, 2, 3, 4), 67 (tr & bl), 69 (1, 2, 3, 4), 71, 75, 77br, 79 (tl, tr, & br), 81br, 83 (tr & b), 88, 89 (t & b), 100–101, 102, 104 (ct, cb, & b), 105 (t, cb, & b), 106, 107t, 108 (t, c, & b), 111 (ct & b), 112b, 113 (t & b), 114t, 115 (t & b), 117, 118 (t, c, & b), 119t, 121 (tl, tr, & b), 122 (t, c & b), 123 (t, c, & b), 124, 125t, 126 (t, c & b), 127 (t & b), 134 (bl & br), 135 (tl & br), 136 (l, tr & br), 137, 138 (l, c & r), 139, 140, 143 (tr, bl & br), 145, 146–147, 149 (t, bl & br), 156, 159 (a, b, c, d, e), 164–165, 167, 172–173 (a, b, c, d, e, f), 177fr, 179 (1, 2, 3, 4), 180–181 (1, 2, 3, 4), 189 (a, b, c, d), 190–191 (a, b, c, d, e, f, g, h), 193 (a, b, c, e, f, g, h), 194 (b & c), 197 (t, br & fr), 198–199 (a, c, d), 205 (t & b), 206–207.

All other images © Dorling Kindersley
For further information see: www.dkimages.com

DK LONDON

Editor Anna Kruger
Editorial Assistant Lucy Philpott
Designer Geoff Borin
Senior Designer Glenda Fisher
Managing Editor Ruth O'Rourke
Managing Art Editor Marianne Markham
Production Editor Tony Phipps
Production Controller Stephanie McConnell
Jacket Designer Amy Cox
Jacket Coordinator Jasmin Lennie
Art Director Maxine Pedliham
Publishing Director Katie Cowan

Photography Jason Ingram, Huw Richards

First published in Great Britain in 2022
by Dorling Kindersley Limited
DK, One Embassy Gardens, 8 Viaduct Gardens,
London, SW11 7BW

The authorized representative in the EEA is
Dorling Kindersley Verlag GmbH. Arnulfstr. 124,
80636 Munich, Germany

Copyright © 2022 Dorling Kindersley Limited
A Penguin Random House Company
10 9 8 7 6 5 4 3 2
003–322787–Mar/2022

A CIP catalogue record for this book
is available from the British Library.
ISBN: 978-0-2414-8132-5

Printed and bound in Italy

For the curious
www.dk.com

This book was made with Forest Stewardship
Council ™ certified paper – one small step in
DK's commitment to a sustainable future.

For more information go to www.dk.com/our-green-pledge

ABOUT THE AUTHOR

In 1999, Huw Richards moved from Yorkshire to mid-west Wales with his parents, who were after "the good life". At three years old, Huw was helping his parents in the vegetable garden. Aged twelve, he created his own YouTube channel, Huw Richards, about vegetable gardening. He now has over 500,000 YouTube subscribers and his videos have collectively been viewed over 50 million times, including via Facebook.

Ever since, Huw has set out to help people reconnect with the food they eat and to empower them to grow their own food. With over 15 years' growing experience using organic and permaculture principles, Huw launched Abundance Academy in 2020, providing online courses on improving garden productivity. He has also set up Regenerative Media, connecting the public with sustainable and inspirational farmers, growers, and producers.

Huw has been featured in *The Times*, *The Guardian*, and on BBC News. He has also appeared live on BBC's *The One Show*. In 2020, Huw released his second book *Grow Food For Free* following the success of his debut *Veg in One Bed*, also published by DK.

If he isn't in the garden or testing out new camera gear, Huw can be found in the kitchen, pursuing his newfound passion of cooking.

Huw can also be found on **Instagram at @huwsgarden.**